THE NATURE OF
THE SOCIAL STUDIES

by

Robert Barr, Associate Professor
Department of Education
Indiana University

James L. Barth, Associate Professor
Department of Education
Purdue University

S. Samuel Shermis, Associate Professor
Department of Education
Purdue University

With Foreword by
Edgar B. Wesley

An ETC Publication

C | P

Library of Congress Cataloging in Publication Data

Barr, Robert D.
  The nature of the social studies.

  1. Social sciences — Study and Teaching I. Barth,
James L., 1931-   joint author. II. Shermis, S. Samuel,
joint author. III. Title.

H61.B257   300'.7   77-2014
ISBN o-88280-049-3

Copyright © 1978 by ETC Publications
                Palm Springs
                California 92262

TABLE OF CONTENTS

FOREWORD

by

Edgar Bruce Wesley

The field of the social studies has long suffered from conflicting definitions, an overlapping of functions, and a confusion of philosophies. These variations have resulted not so much in errors and mistakes as in diffusion and weakness. They have introduced uncertainties; they have perpetuated indecision; they have hindered unification; they have delayed progress.

The phrase "social studies" has been defined as social sciences, as social service, as socialism, as radical left-wing thinking, as social reform, as anti-history, as a unification of social subjects, as a field, as a federation, as an integrated curriculum, as pro-child reform, as curriculum innovation. Elements of truth may be found in each of these concepts. No other subject has suffered such divisive doctrines. While other areas may involve combinations of various disciplines, none of them leads to the confusion that exists in the social studies.

Many attempts to achieve unity and agreement in the social studies have been made. Committees, organizations, and individuals have advocated various names, terms phrases, and changes. For example, for a time "social education" was proposed as a substitute phrase. At other times the complete elimination, even the downright suppression of the phrase was advocated. At one time, a State Superintendent of Education in California officially banned the use of the phrase, insisting that the proper term was *social science*. Still the argument, the wrangle, the discussion, the babel of conflicting voices continue. The attempts to achieve unity in philosophy, in method, in evaluation, and terminology have at best achieved only local and temporary success.

Finally in November, 1970, a practical and appealing proposal appeared on the horizon. A forthright article appeared in *Social Education*, the journal of the National Council for the Social Studies, proposing a recognition and acceptance of a three-part solution to the dilemma of conflicting utterances. James L. Barth and S. Samuel Shermis, both of Purdue University, proposed that we accept actualities and recognize that social studies may be perceived as (1) citizenship training, (2) as the social sciences altered for instructional purposes and (3) as reflective inquiry. This proposal won immediate attention. It was accepted by some as a realistic description and an incisive analysis of the realities. Fortunately, these two educators, with the help of Professor Robert Barr of Indiana University, have expanded and recorded in detail this unique proposal. I am happy to add my voice to that of my three colleagues and in a few condensed pages to summarize its meaning and comment upon its potentialities.

The heart of the social studies is relationships — relationships primarily between and among human beings. Perhaps the full significance of this word can best be understood by a brief overview of the whole curriculum. In doing so one perceives (1) that *things* are assigned to *science*, (2) that *quantification* is assigned to *mathematics*, (3) that *communication* is assigned to *English*, (4) that *creativity* is assigned to *art*, (5) that *work* is assigned to *vocations*, (6) that *location* is assigned to *geography*, (7) that *leisure* is assigned to *recreation* and (8) that *relationships* is assigned to the *social studies*.

Yet one immediately perceives that human relationships is both too inclusive and too vague to be encompassed within the term "social studies." The individual person may be of interest to doctors, preachers, and psychologists, but the single person does not constitute the major concern of the social studies until he establishes a network of relationships with at least one other person. Naturally he also joins groups, organizations, institutions and in turn these create a seamless web of human relations. They constitute the heart and the essence of the social studies.

To facilitate organization and study, the social studies have been divided into various subjects and aspects. The long story of past relations is assigned to history, material relations are assigned to economics and the various other aspects are assigned to different subdivisions of the social studies. Curiously enough, these various parts have never been integrated or merged satisfactorily into an accepted or recognized whole. The sum total of the parts does not equal the whole; unclassified portions of the field lie outside extant subjects. Hence the various attempts to define the field have gained only partial success. This book by Barr, Barth, and Shermis is perhaps the most promising effort to effect a consensus or agreement as to the unity of the field of social studies.

The whole book is enriched and embellished by two original chapters. The first consists of a simulated conversation in a teachers' room in which a young intern is trying earnestly to understand the imprecise terminology and the contradictory ideas that swirl through the atmosphere. The banter and humor of this chapter are convincing and the mystifying "explanations" with which the teachers instruct the intern sound faithful to reality. The teachers leave her as perplexed as when she entered the room. The rest of the book is a clarification of the jumbled talk that polluted that pedagogical coffee room.

The other unique chapter is entitled "Check Yourself Out." The reader who takes this inventory will probably still be unsatisfied with himself (and probably the test too) but he or she will have acquired some specific understanding of social studies terminology and assuredly he will be somewhat mindful of his confusions and beliefs and his status within the profession. They will also be much more firmly grounded in the three fundamental steps of (1) purpose, (2) method, and (3) content. They may even have reached at least tentatively a conclusion as to which tradition they are now willing to identify themselves. By means of this formal inventory, the authors have cleverly made fellow-collaborators out of their readers, thus achieving Ranke's famous formula which asks for the transformation of students into colleagues. This chapter provides a measure of the success of the whole book. The authors have thus demonstrated courage by holding a mirror before the faces of their readers and thus running the risk of their disapproval. However successful the test may be as a measuring instrument, it is a shrewdly designed technique of teaching, persuading, and convincing.

The structure of this book is clear, simple, and appealing. One by one, the three main traditions (Social Studies taught as Citizenship Transmission, Social Studies taught as Social Science, Social Studies taught as Reflective Inquiry) are described in considerable detail; their development and growth are narrated; their status estimated and their prospects forecast; their supporters identified and their strengths and weaknesses are enumerated. Interwoven into these descriptive analyses are the three basic concepts which the authors believe to be (1) purpose, (2) method, and (3) content. Despite the authors' disclaimer that they are not writing a book on how to teach the social studies, they nevertheless make a contribution toward the enrichment of the teaching process.

The tradition of Social Studies taught as Citizenship Transmission as the prime theme in the teaching of the social studies naturally comes up for first consideration. The evolution of the tradition is contemporary with the evolution of the republic itself. The Declaration of Independence, the Constitution, and other revolutionary documents became the early civics and history. Among the influential factors contributing to the growth of Citizenship Transmission are its simplicity and directness, the curriculum laws of the various states, the generous sums of money spent on schools, the land grants from the public domain dedicated to education, the close association of public education and democracy. All these contributed to the strength, endurance, dominance, and popularity of the citizenship tradition.

The Social Studies taught as Social Science is the second great tradition. The authors' description of this tradition is historical, precise, adequate and convincing. The distinction between the *sciences* and the *studies* advocated by Wesley[1] greatly facilitated discussion and this detailed lists and dates of founders, books, magazines, organizations, events, and especially methods forecast the tremendous growth of the 1960's that characterized the participation in the school curriculum by social science organizations. Previous to 1900, only historians paid formal attention to the school program. The entry of social science organizations greatly enriched the number of scholars interested in the teaching of social studies.

The theory and practice of Social Studies taught as Reflective Inquiry is the third tradition in the development of the social studies. The authors trace with a touch of nostalgic sadness its questionable ancestry, its murky companions, and saddest of all, its half-hearted and belated acceptance. They characterize our society as overwhelmed by change, smothered underneath accumulating knowledge, burdened with conflict, and rescued, at least temporarily, by some consensus.

How can we transmit values amid swirls of change and how can we select among pluralistic and conflicting heritages what is appropriate for now, much less tomorrow? After many delays amid competing proposals, some have concluded that the process of Reflective Inquiry offers one of the most promising alternatives available in the social studies field. John Dewey, the godfather of Reflective Inquiry, rejected the superficial transmission of culture and of the academic disciplines as the proper functions of education. Instead he advocated the selection and study of contemporary problems and issues that are important to society and that appeal to students.

The authors trace the slow acceptance of Reflective Inquiry and explain how various attempts to promote understanding were subverted into the traditional practices of assignment, drill, recitation, and examination. Scholars, critics, writers, and many parents scorned the study of current events, problem solving, decision making, the examination of controversial issues, and the application of criteria by teachers and students. Teachers continued their traditional content-minded ways, continuing to place their emphasis upon memorizing facts rather than upon the acquisition and application of skills and individual and social development. Fortunately, a number of progressive scholars such as Metcalf, Oliver, Wronski, Shaver, and Engle have demonstrated how students learn and how to break the old deadly routine of custom. And this work is a major contribution because it explores the meaning of social studies. In fact it may become a landmark, a turning point in the history of the teaching of the social studies.

[1]Edgar Bruce Wesley, *Teaching the Social Studies* (Boston, 1937), Chapter II. A somewhat enlarged version of this treatment appears in the appendix to the second edition, 1942.

PREFACE

This book grows out of what have been a persistent puzzle to the authors, all of whom have been social studies educators for a number of years. The puzzle concerns word magic. Over a long period of time, whenever social studies teachers talked, there seemed to be a problem of communication. To be sure, everyone employed the "same" words -- "citizenship," "thinking," "values," "problem-solving," and the like. But it was clear that social studies educators did not share the same association of meanings for these words.

Awareness of this communication problem deepened as we worked with teachers in university classes, institutes, workshops, clinics, and in-service presentations. Everyone agreed upon the importance of "inquiry," everyone wanted to be "relevant" and to promote "decision-making." But when all was said and done, teachers returned to their classes but little changed.

Slowly we came to see that teachers were practicing what they interpreted certain words to mean. Often their interpretation was far removed from what was stressed in institutes and workshops. Our point of view seemed to be transformed by teachers into something very different, even though teachers avowed the same words and principles. When it finally became clear to us what had happened, that surface agreement often concealed deep philosophical disagreements, we set out to understand and explain this paradox. This book is the culmination of our inquiry.

This book, which slowly developed during the first half of the 1970's, is grounded in the realities of social studies teaching--not the ideals to which everyone obviously assented, but actual classroom behavior. Some, of course, will criticize us for focusing on what *is* in the social studies rather than what should be. But we believe that it is defensible to analyze the field as it is and was. And when we examined classroom behavior, what we saw was a lack of focus, goals out of step with practices and, most important, teachers without a clear sense of identity. But this was not surprising, for the social studies has been a stage upon which virtually everyone in our society has urged very different roles. Scholars from the social sciences vigorously encouraged teachers to instruct the young in the ways of their disciplines. Spokesmen from civic groups, organized labor, industry--virtually everyone with a point of view or a cause--assumed that the schools in general and social studies in particular provided a forum for their unique brand of social philosophy. And throughout it all, many talked of the necessity for inquiry, problem-solving, and preparation for citizenship. The net result is that the social studies became all things to all men.

In addition to the diverse forces pressing upon social studies teachers from the outside, the teachers themselves also brought with them a variety of different preparations. Many were trained in history, some in sociology, and the other social sciences; some even came with little or no background in any of the social sciences. The diversity of forces operating within and without the profession created a paradox: while everyone agreed that social studies necessarily integrates knowledge, values, and skills from many sources for the purpose of citizenship education, there has been little or no consensus about the proper means of providing such integration.

Almost everyone believes that the purpose of social studies is citizenship education, but for 60 years educators in our field have not agreed on what it means to prepare a good citizen. In fact, just the opposite has occurred; for the field has been cluttered with different and often conflicting interpretations regarding good citizenship. In the past there has been a continuing battle within the social studies about whose definition is correct. During recent years, the authors of this book began to see that it was useful to view the various factions, points of view, and conflicts as subsets of the larger field rather than "either-or" confrontations. As we began to view the various positions in the field from a larger perspective, a more general, and we think, more useful approach to defining the field began to emerge. We believe that social studies serves as an advanced organizer for the integration of history, social sciences, and the humanities for the purpose of citizenship education. Since the turn of the century, as scholars have sought the "best" means of integrating social studies, three very different perspectives began to emerge. As these perspectives have evolved through the decades, three very clear traditions have emerged in the field. We have labeled these traditions "Social Studies Taught as Citizenship Transmission," "Social Studies Taught as Social Science" and "Social Studies Taught as Reflective Inquiry."

The purpose of dividing our analysis in such a manner is, first, to summarize the disparate traditions in the social studies, and, second, to help future teachers as well as practicing ones clarify their own understanding of the field. It is clear to us that all too often social studies teachers lack a clear and persuasive identity. Such an identity comes about only by reflecting upon values, by thinking about what one stands for. We wish to invite you to an understanding of the field of social studies, to learn about its traditions, and finally to make up your own mind about the way you think citizenship ought to be taught.

Robert Barr   James L. Barth   S. Samuel Shermis

DEDICATION

To Beryl Barr, Martha and Raymond Barth, and to Harry and Celia Shermis, this book, a small payment on a large debt, is fondly dedicated.

"Man, I've had it!"

"What's wrong, Parker, it's only third period."

"If you guys had the kind of third period DeeDee wished on me, you'd be whipped too."

Parker glanced around the room, seeking an expression of sympathy. He found none. This did not deter him. He continued his litany.

"What am I supposed to do with them? Hell, they can't even read. And if DeeDee Brown doesn't stop waving her cute little something around in class, by God, we'll be filming an X-rated flick."

At the mention of DeeDee's name, Mrs. Wilhelm looked up. She put her knitting down and asked mildly, "Jim, are you having trouble with DeeDee?"

"Am I having trouble with DeeDee?" he repeated. "I can't get her to do a lick of work. She's either flirting with Big George or she's sharpening her pencil or doing whatever else she's not supposed to."

"Well, I never had trouble with DeeDee." Mrs. Wilhelm responded softly, with the emphasis on just the first person pronoun.

Mr. Parker leered at her briefly and thought to himself, "And if I had your body, I wouldn't have trouble with my students either." However, he said nothing. Katherine Wilhelm, having shared the coffee lounge for three years with James Parker, flushed slightly, but persisted.

"Now, Jim, I know that DeeDee is a very attractive girl, but it is possible to reach her. Once you get her interested in something, she'll do very nice work. Really."

1

"Kathy, she's been in this class for two months now, and frankly, I don't think I can do much about her interests. Not and keep my job."

Kathy Wilhelm flushed again, thinking to herself, "He says that sort of thing just to embarrass me. I must stop giving him the satisfaction."

Laurie Townsley, an intern with the Social Studies Department of the Millard Fillmore Junior-Senior High School of one week's tenure, sat and listened. Since she had opened her mouth the first day and been dismissed as naive, conventionally idealistic, and liberal, she had kept her own counsel. The topic of the discussion was scarcely novel, but she was interested in Mrs. Wilhelm's response to Mr. Parker.

"Jim, I don't want to argue with you, but I had DeeDee last year, and I know that she is capable of doing fine work. You have to make an effort to find out what she's really ...."

"Yeah, Kathy, I know. What she's interested in."

"What she's interested in," thought Laurie. "That doesn't sound much like Mr. Davis' ideas."

She thought back to her interview with the principal three days before. After a two minute "We're-so-glad-to-have-you-welcome-to-the-faculty" speech, Mr. Davis got down to the issues at hand.

"Now I am going to be very straight about this, and I want you to be sure and understand. I run a tight ship here, and I will insist that you do likewise when you start teaching. These kids will run over you if you give them half a chance. As an intern, they'll give you pure hell until they have tested you. So, don't give them a chance. Be on top of the situation from the first day or you won't last long." He swiveled sideways and gazed out the window. "Now, there's one other thing," he began. "You're a social studies intern. Your job here is to teach these kids to respect their country and grow up to be good citizens. Now that's a hell of an important job, but it's also a hell of a hard job." He turned and leveled a piercing gaze straight into Laurie's eyes. It was a look obviously left over from his years as a coach; a look originally developed for a fullback about to be sent in on third and six, inside the ten yard line.

2

"The people in this community feel very strongly about citizenship." His eyes bored in with the message. "They expect us to mold these kids, to teach them proper behavior and respect for authority, to obey the laws, and to be clean and neat. We have no place for cynics and pessimists; this is a great country and we have got to inspire these kids to live up to its highest ideals. And with this rowdy bunch, that's quite a challenge. You have the chance to teach them about our forefathers, and the Constitution, and about the wars we have won. It's a great opportunity . . .."

With a start, Laurie returned to the conversation flowing around her in the teacher's room, just as Ben Kravitz, who had been stapling examination sheets in the corner, spoke up.

"Well, as far as I am concerned, this school system hired me to teach American history and that's just what I'm doing, five days a week, nine months out of the year. I do the best job I can to present history, but if a kid doesn't want to learn, well, there's nothing I can do."

Laurie forgot herself and blurted out, "Mr. Kravitz, do you mean won't learn, or can't learn?

Ben Kravitz stopping stapling and looked at Laurie, unable to decide if the unspoken intention was critical. He decided to play it safe. "What do you mean, Miss Townsley?"

"Um, I was just wondering if you thought that students can't learn because they're not bright enough, or they don't learn because they don't find anything interesting in the material, or if they are just contrary?"

"Hostile," Mr. Kravitz reassured himself. "Damn college kids. It was those educational method classes they were getting now. What those college professors really needed was to have to teach in a high school classroom, day in and day out like he did. Then they would change their tune."

"Miss Townsley, there are a good many children in this school who really don't belong here. They don't have the ability, the interest, or the desire to study. What they need is a good course or two in vocational education. Frankly, I doubt that they can really benefit from my course in history, as important as the subject is."

3

"Mr. Kravitz, I know I'm new and all that, but I just don't see how you could say that. As far as I am concerned, every student needs social studies if they are going to function effectively as a citizen in a democracy."

Kathy Wilhelm smiled and nodded agreement. Mr. Kravitz said nothing, confirmed in his opinion that Laurie Townsley subscribed to the usual platitudes. A teacher was assigned to a subject to teach; that was what he was paid to do and there was little point in theoretical bullsessions.

Jim Parker had, by this time, drifted away from the conversation, turned on his transistor radio and began noting the ball scores. This was, after all, a more substantial concern. All he had really intended to do in the first place was to let off steam and he wondered why everybody had gotten off on a discussion that sounded suspiciously intellectual.

Arthur Leonard chose that moment to enter the coffeeroom. He sized up the situation in a few seconds and asked cheerfully, "Well, how is everyone?"

The stiff nods and murmurs, "Hello, Art, how are 'ya?", confirmed his suspicious. However, he told himself, whatever had arisen was not of his making. He might as well expend his energies on preparing for his next class, "A Study of Man." Laurie was happy to see Mr. Leonard; in fact, she was just waiting for the time he would stop calling her Miss Townsley and invite her to call him Art. Art, she thought, was the nearest thing to a social scientist in this department. He was not only good looking but his M.A. in anthropology confirmed even further her high opinion of him.

Mr. Leonard began to transfer a map of the Plains Arapesh onto a transparency. "A Study of Man," as far as Mr. Leonard was concerned, was the only viable social studies class being taught in this school. The collection of tired old men, do-gooders, and jocks masquerading as teachers had about as much conception of the social studies as he had of trigonometric functions. He glanced at Laurie Townsley out of the corner of his eye. As long as she wasn't doing anything, why couldn't he ask her to help him with the transparency? This would free him to do something a little less pedestrian. Nothing wrong with

4

preparing the multi-color charts on the Arapesh, but the intern could do that while he worked on the next unit.

"Miss Townsley, would you like to help me with this work?" Actually, he convinced himself, he was doing her a favor. If she got involved in curriculum making for "A Study of Man," she would learn something and perhaps justify the internship expense the school had committed itself to.

"Why, yes, Mr. Leonard. I'd be happy to."

"Well, let me explain what this is." The other teachers had by now returned to their occupations, Mr. Kravitz stapling, Mrs. Wilhelm knitting, and Jim Parker listening to his transistor radio.

"Yes, please do. This all looks interesting. I've been meaning to speak to you about this course, but I just haven't had time."

"Well, I think it's really something you'd enjoy doing. It has more potential for teaching critical thinking than anything else I can think of." The assertion was designed to be overheard by his fellow teachers, and in fact they did not miss it. Only Kathy Wilhelm looked up, without any expression. Mr. Kravitz continued to staple and Jim Parker held the radio close to his left ear, clucking and wincing as the plays were described.

"Yes, Mr. Leonard. Dr. Myers, my University supervisor, is very much in favor of critical thinking."

"I know, I've heard him a time or two. However, I'd like his viewpoint more if he were tuned onto some of the more exciting innovations in the last few years. I don't happen to think that his ideas are going to generate any critical thinking, although," he hastened to add as he noticed that Laurie tightened the corners of her mouth, "of course, I'm certain that Dr. Myers is just as sincere as I am."

Arthur Leonard, convinced that he had an attentive audience in the young intern, began to speak enthusiastically.

"You know, 'The Study of Man' is a hell of a course if I do say so myself. I'm really teaching these kids something very important to them. The course is based on the assumption that students can learn to think critically by observing the inquiry process of social scientists. We study the Arapesh tribe of New Guinea, and my students really get involved. They actually learn anthropology, not just second hand, but by seeing how a

5

primitive society works; how the members live, how they raise children. They learn anthropology by doing many of the same things real anthropologists do. I'm really very committed to this idea. I think the best way to train youth effectively is to teach them to think scientifically. and that means to follow the day-to-day information-gathering techniques of the social scientist. I'm an anthropologist, and I want my students to learn to think and act the way an anthropologist acts. If I were a political scientist or sociologist or even a historian, I would feel the kids should think their way also.

"Well, I agree on one thing," Laurie interjected, "my professors say that students should be taught the skills of critical thinking, but I'm not really sure that teaching kids to be social scientists is the answer. I guess I'm more inclined to focus on student interest and problems."

"Why don't you just forget that crap they fed you at the Teachers College about social studies teaching?" A trace of disgust crept into Leonard's voice.

"Those education professors haven't been in a classroom for ten years. You're not a social studies teacher, you're a history teacher. Teach your students historiography -- use primary resources, teach them to validate evidence, draw conclusions. Let them do the things that historians do -- what could be more useful?"

Laurie frowned, thinking that she would have to set Mr. Leonard straight. She wasn't just a history teacher. Her interests were broader than that. But just then the intercom squawked, causing all of the teachers to start.

"If Miss Townsley is there, I'd like to talk with her for just a moment, if it's convenient.

Mr. Leonard looked at Laurie. Laurie returned the stare. She knew neither the voice nor the reason for the request. "That's Syzmanowski, the vice principal. He is requesting the honor of your presence."

"What have I done? I can't think of . . . ."

Noting her anxiety, Leonard reassured her immediately. "Nothing, Laurie. He is probably going to interview you about something. He does this with all new interns."Laurie excused herself and walked to the main office.

6

Mr. Syzmanowski, looked up, smiled briefly and rose from his desk to shake hands. "I'm glad to get this chance to talk to you." He settled back into his chair behind a massive and cluttered desk. "One of the reasons we agreed to have an intern here at Fillmore High is that we want to innovate. In the last few years we have made good progress. We've already introduced BSCS and Chemstudy to the science curriculum." The words meant nothing to Laurie, although she surmised that both were experimental science programs. "Unfortunately," the vice-principal continued, " the social studies people are, uh . . . a bit hesitant to try anything really innovative, and so we have been trying to interest them in some new programs."

As Szymanowski continued to talk, he begin hinting that the six teachers in the social studies department had been unwilling and uncooperative in efforts at innovation. It seemed that they sat aside and allowed their colleagues in science, mathematics, and English to experiment with new curriculum programs while they themselves had done nothing.

"Mind you, our social studies people are all very fine and really excellent teachers." The vice-principal had a nervous habit of tapping a pencil on his desk as he talked.

"All of them are very conscientious. All of them are good teachers but they are individualists. So individual, in fact, they seem never to agree on anything. I think you will find Mr. Leonard one of our strongest teachers. Art Leonard has an M.A. in anthropology and his course, 'A Study of Man', is first-rate. Before he joined the faculty two years ago, our 10th grade world history course was absolutely the worst course in our curriculum. Art has replaced the survey history course with a really fine course in anthropology. He has his students acting like junior anthropologists before the year is out. Now I don't mean to imply that the other social studies teachers are not trying, that's the last thing I would do." His pencil tapping continued.

"Now take Mr. Parker for example . . .." He paused for a moment and then continued, "Parker is certainly not as sophisticated as the other social studies teachers, but he's a fine teacher. He works extremely well with our students. He's probably had more influence on young people out of class than

7

most teachers have in class. Another good teacher is Miss Goodrich; but rather than solid curriculum development, she emphasizes current events, student projects, and the like." His staccato tapping pounded to a crescendo.

"The other teachers are as solid as a rock, but it is all text-book and lecture. And when they get together it's like a D.A.R. meeting. Well, Miss Townsley, we would like you to have a good experience here. And at the same time we want you to help us. What we want you to do . . ." he hesitated.

"What we want you to do is to decide which teacher you want to team with, and then see me again so that we can again talk about some of your ideas and innovations in social studies. I would also like for you to visit the elementary school in our complex. It's only a short walk across the campus, and I've already talked to Mrs. Freeman about letting you observe her 4th grade social studies class and to talk with her and a few other teachers. You might even identify one of the elementary teachers to work with occasionally. I believe it's very important for you to be familiar with our entire K-12 social studies program. I think you will discover that some of the most creative teaching is found in the elementary grades."

Mr. Syzmanowski finished, smiled, rose briskly and ushered her out. The interview was over. Laurie was confused, even though the request was fairly simple and straightforward. What, she asked herself, was the purpose of asking an utterly inexperienced intern to work on creating innovations? And what did she know about elementary schools? Where was the leadership in the department? Why had the social studies people resisted introducing new materials when the biology and math teachers had been innovating for a number of years? And, most interestingly, why did the push for innovation come from the vice-principal, instead of the teachers? From what little she knew about schools, administrators were supposed to be the real obstacles to progress. Very clearly, in this school at least, teachers were the obstacles and it was the vice-principal who was trying to light a fire under the department.

As she left the office, Laurie decided that the best course of action lay in calling her university supervisor, Dr. Myers. He would be able to advise her. She went to the teachers' lounge,

8

which was now empty, and dialed Dr. Myer's office. Surprisingly, he answered immediately. Laurie explained the situation to him. He listened and asked a few questions.

"Laurie, I think this is a potentially good experience for you, and you are lucky in being allowed to choose the teacher with whom you want to work, and some observations at the elementary level should prove especially worthwhile. I'm not going to tell you with whom to work, but I'll give you some questions you might ask."

Myers continued. "Try to find out from each of them why he teaches social studies. You remember, we talked about the purpose of social studies? Then, try to find out what he chooses for content. Then ask about the kind of method and techniques he employs. If you can get straight answers to these three questions . . . "

They continued talking, with Laurie asking questions, attempting to get Dr. Myers to elaborate on his directions to her. Finally, she began to talk about what was really bothering her.

"Dr. Myers, you know something kind of uh, gets to me. In all of our classroom discussions, we talked about these three. We went over and over purpose, content, and method. The readings, the textbook, you -- all said the same thing. Social studies is supposed to get kids to think critically. It's supposed to deal with social problems. It's supposed to deal with citizenship, decision-making and that sort of thing."

Laurie stopped for a moment. Dr. Myers interposed a noncommital "uh huh."

"Well, I just don't see this. Any of this. These kids aren't dealing with problems, and no one is asking them to make a decision."

Dr. Myers sighed. He had listened to the same complaint dozens, perhaps hundreds of times before. It was difficult to explain. Nothing he had ever said really convinced his students that he wasn't a cloud-bound intellectual who didn't have any notion of what was really happening in schools. However, once again he tried to explain his position to Laurie. The position he advocated -- problem-solving, decision-making, "all that stuff," as his students would say -- was indeed not found in actual practice. Teachers, for the most part, simply transmitted their own

9

convictions -- although they thought of them as the true will of the community -- to their students. A few, like Arthur Leonard, were basically social scientists, who, although they talked about problem-solving and critical thinking, were still oriented to the thinking of a particular discipline.

Laurie listened to his explanation politely. Intellectually, she could follow Myers and agree with him. But, the problem still did not evaporate. If social studies were truly concerned with getting kids to think critically about problem areas, and if all of the books agreed on this, why were classroom teachers so far removed from Holy Writ? Nevertheless, Laurie thought to herself that she would attempt to ask the teachers the questions Dr. Myers recommended.

As she hung up the phone and glanced at her watch, Laurie realized that school would be out soon and she might have a better chance of catching the teachers with a little free time. So she sat down and looked over the handbook and schedules of Fillmore High until the final bell rang.

As the last students were clearing the halls, Laurie went upstairs to the social studies preparation area.

In the room, which was really a combination storage room, duplicating area and coffee lounge, Laurie found Art Leonard. Immediately she asked him the questions suggested by Dr. Myers. For what purpose, she asked, should the social studies be taught?

"Well, Laurie, the only rationale for teaching the social studies is to train for citizenship, and the only way to train really responsible citizens is to get them to be the kind of people who make decisions responsibly."

That sounded good to Laurie. How, she then asked, was this to be done?

"The best way to train persons to think about social problems is to get them to think scientifically. And that means to follow the intellectual procedures of the social scientists. If you want people to discover ideas about social change, why not get them to see how anthropologists and sociologists, just to mention two, think about social change?"

Laurie thought, "How would you go about doing this?"

"Well, you saw my materials on preliterate tribes, didn't you?"

Mr. Leonard went on to talk, with renewed animation, about the benefits to be gained in studying about the Arapesh, their folkways, and the issue of social change in a preliterate society.

Laurie asked a few more questions. Then she excused herself to find the others. For some reason, her original enthusiasm for Arthur Leonard's anthropology curriculum was beginning to fade. She could not disagree with Leonard's convictions about the need to train for responsible citizenship. What else was social studies for? Nor could she argue with his convictions about intellectual training. But it was beginning to become difficult for her to see how looking at the Arapesh through an anthropologist's eyes was good preparation for citizenship. Still, Leonard was no fool, and his ideas would bear closer examination.

She found herself between the rooms of Mr. Kravitz and Mrs. Wilhelm. She looked both ways, found the two teachers at their desks, and decided, for no good reason, to see Mr. Kravitz first.

She politely greeted the neatly groomed, gentle, and tired man. Without mentioning either her discussion with Dr. Myers or Arthur Leonard, Laurie explained that she wanted to hear Mr. Kravitz's "philosophy" of social studies. Whether that was the right word for Kravitz's feelings was another question, but teachers were forever talking about a philosophy of this and a philosophy of that. "What is your purpose for teaching social studies, Mr. Kravitz?"

"Why is social studies taught? Well, my dear, that's a good question. The answer is to prepare young people to be good citizens."

That, Laurie thought to herself, was exactly what Art Leonard had said. Could this conventional, colorless man be in agreement with Leonard?

"Mr. Kravitz, could you tell me what you mean by 'good citizen'?"

Kravitz thought for a moment and continued. "A good citizen is one who behaves like one. He votes. He knows and obeys the laws, is responsible, fulfills his civic obligations. And he participates in civic activity."

No. Clearly Kravitz and Leonard were not talking about the same thing. Leonard's explanation identified citizenship in ter-

11

ms of problem-solving. Kravitz was talking about something entirely different.

"Mr. Kravitz, how do you go about training for good citizenship?" This was perhaps the way to get at what Dr. Myers spoke of as the what or perhaps the how of teaching.

Kravitz again thought for a moment, but only a moment. Apparently he had answered questions like this before. His responses had a memorized quality about them.

"Well, my dear, students need to know certain kinds of information in order to be good citizens. They need to know the history of their country, how the government works, and things like that. We want to teach them what they will need to know when they get out of here and have to take their place in the real world."

Kathy Wilhelm materialized out of nowhere. "Are we continuing our little discussion of a while back? What's happening?"

She apparently had been listening, but since their rooms were so close to each other, this was scarcely eavesdropping. Laurie found out that Mrs. Wilhelm had nothing really to add to Kravitz's explanation. Mrs. Wilhelm returned to her earlier desire that teachers should make social studies interesting to students. High school social studies was indeed designed to prepare students to be good citizens, people who could cope with problems "out in the real world" she repeated Kravitz's phrase. Wasn't high school part of this "real world?" Laurie wondered to herself.

As Kathy Wilhelm left the room, Laurie wandered on down the hall and into Connie Goodrich's classroom. Connie was engrossed in arranging a bulletin board collage representing the major events of recent years. She had a pencil stuck behind her ear and a mouth full of thumb tacks and in a down to earth, disheveled sort of way she was attractive. She invited Laurie and Kathy to join her and Marge Johnson in some coffee.

"Keep us company while I finish this bulletin board."

Before Laurie could ask her set of questions, Art Leonard and Jim Parker walked in.

"What's this, a party?"

"Sure, if there's any coffee left. Join us."

12

The talk was desultory until Connie turned to Laurie.

"Hey, I understand that you have been working with Dr. Myers in the College of Education. He really had an impact on me. Especially his techniques at value clarification and analysis. Before I took his class, I had never thought of doing things like that in a classroom; now they are the major emphasis of my government course."

"Oh, Connie, you're not still doing all those gimmicky value lessons? I thought you would grow out of all of that."

"Marge, what could possibly be more worthwhile than to help kids gain an understanding of their own values."

Marge finished off her coffee and began screwing the top on her thermos. "I'll tell you what can be more worthwhile, to *teach* them values. These kids don't have any of their own. With all the governmental scandal and corruption around, I am absolutely convinced that we have just got to teach our students basic moral and ethical principles. The newspapers are one long nightmare of unprincipled, amoral men who wallow in their selfish goals." Her tone rose to the occasion, "I'm sick of all this value clarification. We all know there are certain standards of right and wrong; good and bad, and we damn well better teach them."

"Oh Marjorie," Art Leonard interrupted Connie's reply and intruded into the discussion. "You sound like an evangelistic preacher. Billy Graham Johnson -- in the flesh. Come on now, both of you are wrong to muddle around with students' values. That's the responsibility of the home and the church. Our job is to try to be objective; teach some scientific skills, and leave the values alone."

Jim Parker was listening to his ball game again, holding his radio close to his ear. "Kids today don't give a damn about anything except pimples, petting, and the P.S.A.T."

Katherine Wilhelm was obviously disturbed by the discussion. She shook her head in disapproval while she took out her knitting from an oversized purse beside her chair. Art Leonard could not help but taunt her. "Katherine, you're just as bad as the rest. With all that God and country crap, I've always wondered why you didn't suit out your students in boy-scout uniforms.

"Art, if you spent half as much time being cultured as you do in studying culture, you would be much better off. You can't badger me into an argument." She continued to knit without looking up, but her jaw muscles ground in rhythm with her knitting.

Connie Goodrich turned back toward her finished bulletin board and with a critical frown, surveyed her work. "Well, how do you like it?" A round of approving comments responded, and Laurie finally risked sharing an opinion.

"That's really powerful. Foreign intervention, the CIA and FBI, Federal intervention in state affairs, George Wallace . . .. It sums up everything that has been happening. I hope my teaching can be as exciting as that collage."

Connie walked over and sat down next to the young teacher, while Art Leonard and Marge Johnson continued to argue. "Well," she said, "that bulletin board comes as close to being a course outline as anything. I really try to get my students involved in the controversies that surround us. I want them to think for themselves." She laughed selfconsciously. "I guess that it's a bit presumptious, but I really believe I can help the kids think critically about the issues of the day. I just can't plod through *Magruder's American Government,* studying the separation of powers and the Bill of Rights. They forget it as fast as you teach it." And with a nod toward Art Leonard she softly said, "I also believe it's a cop-out to lock the kids up in a scholarly discipline and spend all your time on theoretical concepts and scholarly inquiry. I can't wait to get the students out surveying political attitudes in the neighborhood and do some opinion polls. The kids love to debate and role-play, and as I have said, we spend a lot of time in the value area."

"I wish I were as positive as you about what I will be doing this year," Laurie replied.

"Oh, I don't know if it's all that good, but I enjoy it." And then with an attentive look Connie asked, "What sort of plans do you have for the coming year?"

14

It was late afternoon the next day. Laurie was still embarrassed by her answer to Connie Goodrich's question. All her comments had sounded little more than idealistic platitudes. "Dumb," she thought later, "did I sound dumb."

Ten minutes later she was sitting alone in the teachers lounge. All the other teachers had gone and she relished the chance to be alone with her thoughts. She had spent most of the day in the nearby elementary school, but the experience only served to compound her confusion and frustration. The three elementary teachers she had observed and talked with were just as varied and contradictory as the secondary teachers.

One fourth grade teacher was obviously Connie Goodrich's elementary counterpart. She was teaching a unit on Feminine Liberation and her students were studing social roles, their own personal prejudices, and their perceptions and misconceptions about women. Laurie smiled when she remembered the teacher having her students switch sexes in a role-playing simulation that proved hilarious yet provoked the class to a heated debate. And even the boys could not explain or defend why the city had a Boy's Club financed by United Fund money and no Girl's Club or even a YWCA. Her purpose for teaching the social studies? She was quick with a reply: to help the kids think for themselves, to explore their own prejudices, personalities, problems, and motives.

The other two elementary teachers both declared adamantly that they were teaching their students to be "good citizens." To them this seemed to mean that their students were to be quiet, respectful, and obedient. They were to "sit up straight and keep their feet on the floor." Still, one of the teachers was just marvelous. She obviously loved history, and in her story hour she had her students thoroughly engrossed with stories about Abe Lincoln. She was a wonderful story teller and was careful to point out a moral that seemed inherent in each story.

The other teacher was "something else." And when she began a loud harangue about what "Good boys and girls should do," Laurie could stand it no longer and quickly slipped out with a shy wave to the teacher.

With a sigh, she pushed herself up from the seat and gathered up her work for the night.

15

She pushed open the school door and stepped out of the stuffy building into the lazy afternoon breeze. The students were lounging on the school steps sharing a cigarette. The boy lying on a basketball leaned his head back and stared upside down at the teacher. "Hey, are you a teacher?"

"Yes," she responded, "I guess I am."

Still watching her upside down, the boy asked, "What do you teach?"

"Well, I'm going to try and teach social studies."

Both boys moaned and their faces twisted in mock agony. The upside down boy now rolled over to face his new found antagonist. "I hate history. It's the most boring subject in school."

"Yeah," joined in the other boy, "social studies sucks."

"Yeah, what kind of social studies you gonna teach?"

Laurie paused and turned back to the boys. "You know," she replied slowly, "I really wish I knew."

CHAPTER 1

The Nature Of The Social Studies

Introduction

Laurie is disturbed, as well might she be. No one would blame her for being resentful, even for calling damnation down upon her entire undergraduate preparation. For in the space of a very few days, Laurie has discovered that (1) her methods instructor's description of social studies has little connection with the realities of classroom teaching, (2) the social studies teachers at Millard Fillmore Junior-Senior High School reflect an almost total inability to communicate with students, and, (3) despite the earnest intentions of the school's administrators, in the final analysis, they have not the slightest idea what direction the department should follow.

Readers should not conclude that in some obscure way social studies teachers are dull, unimaginative, or resistant to change. Nor should it be thought that everyone connected with the enterprise of preparing teachers and teaching students is similarly unable to communicate. The authors would like to propose another explanation.

It appears to us that the central problem lies in the inability of all concerned to see beyond their words. Think for a moment: all of the teachers, administrators, and professors described in the introduction make use of the "same" words. All talk about "social studies," "citizenship," "democracy" and a host of other terms. But it seems obvious that these words do not convey the same meaning to all. The "citizenship" of Mr. Kravitz and Mr. Szymanowski is simply not the same "citizenship" as that of Mrs. Goodrich, Art Leonard, or Dr. Myers.

When the three authors -- all of whom have taught social studies and have been engaged in the preparation of social studies teachers since the mid-1950's --became aware of this disturbing reality, they began to speculate on the underlying issues. Slowly it dawned on us that there is and has been no single entity called the "social studies," for we could identify three distinct and separate traditions, all of which are called "social studies." It then became clear that not only was there no agreement as to the essential nature and purpose of the social studies, there was also little consensus as to desirable content and proper methodology.

As we reflected on this in an article which formed the foundations of this work,[1] it became increasingly apparent that the social studies field lacks a consistent purpose and set of goals. And lacking such clarity, teachers have been unable to decide either upon the best content or most appropriate methods. To be sure, there have been attempts at defining the nature of the social studies and some have been widely quoted.[2] But no one definition was either accepted or used by the practitioners who were teaching social studies to the nation's young people or by the university professors who prepare those same teachers. In order to bring to the field some semblance of identity, we should like to propose a definition.

Social studies is an integration of social sciences and humanities for the purpose of instruction in citizenship education. We emphasize "integration," for social studies is the only field which deliberately attempts to draw upon, in an integrated fashion, the data of the social sciences and the insights of the humanities. We emphasize "citizenship," for social studies, despite the difference in orientation, outlook, purpose, and method of teachers, is almost universally perceived as preparation for citizenship in a democracy.

Although most social studies teachers would probably accept this definition, we suggest that teachers have tended to interpret "integration" in different ways. We suggest that there are patterns by which teachers integrate ideas, information, values, skills, and beliefs. And, upon analysis, we suggest that there are three dominant modes of integration.

In addition to this definition, we now wish to provide you with the core, the thesis of this work. The authors have identified at least three separate and distinct social studies traditions and have argued that teachers *tend* to teach in predictable ways; that these predictable ways form patterns, and that these patterns can be understood and interpreted. The first tradition we call "Citizenship Transmission." This is the oldest tradition in the field, the one which the populace as a whole seems to favor. The

18

essence of this tradition is the deliberate inculcation of what is considered the most desirable knowledge, values, and skills assumed necessary for survival of the culture. The second tradition we call "Social Studies Taught as Social Science" and we assert that this tradition -- at least in its most recent form -- stems from a variety of events which took place in the 1960's. "Social Studies Taught as Social Science" means that teachers wish to acquaint students with the methods of research, the modes of inquiry, and the ways of looking at the world adopted by social scientists. The third tradition we call "Reflective Inquiry." This tradition comes from the philosophy of John Dewey and his followers since the beginning of the 20th Century.

The emphasis in this chapter is on the necessity of preparing students for citizenship. The most important component of citizenship is choice: students will need to identify problems and issues and to make decisions about matters of policy and belief.

At this point, a thoughtful reader might ask, Why do we need a definition of social studies? Of what value is it to think about integrating social studies in terms of the three traditions? Both questions are fair and entirely relevant. The answer is that it is long past time for social studies teachers to think seriously about the important concepts and generalizations in the field. It is necessary for all of the Connie Goodriches, Art Leonards, and Mr. Kravitzes of the teaching profession to cease employing terminology as political slogans and begin thinking beyond the words toward the underlying assumptions. It is, in short, time for serious conceptual clarification, for teachers in the social studies have simply not reached the goals which they have consistently offered to the American people.

There is ample evidence to support the assertion that social studies teachers have not reached goals which they have been projecting for more than seventy years. In 1941, the publication date of the first Purdue Opinion Poll, it was learned -- to continuing surprise and sorrow -- that students who had taken civics and American history courses held beliefs diametrically opposed to the Constitution. Other research has shown that high school graduates are not especially well informed about current events. There is even evidence to demonstrate that, despite the continual exposure to roughly the same material in civics and American history, students are often ignorant of important historical events and of the structure and function of government. The net result, as the American educational philosopher John Dewey noted a half century ago, is to leave citizens to the mercy of all sorts of manipulators and shapers of "public opinion." Indeed, the evidence suggests that Americans tend to think about social issues and political figures in ways which have nothing to do with the model of the rational, deliberate decision-maker so beloved of civics teachers.

In short, the evidence concerning social studies goals is unambiguously consistent: the "products" of 12 years of social studies are too often ignorant when they should be informed, irrational when they should be logical, and illiberal when they should have been guided by the philosophy of our Constitution and Bill of Rights. And at the root of the matter seems to be the persisting difficulty of teachers to think seriously and plan properly in order to reach their cherished goals -- the training of future "citizens" in "problem-solving" and "decision-making" to the end that they can intelligently rule themselves in a political "democracy."

It is for the purpose of thinking in a serious and sustained fashion about the meaning of educational purposes that we now ask you to examine three different ways of conceiving of purposes. We invite you to examine three traditions in the social studies.

Purpose as Conceived by Citizenship Transmitters

Do you remember the introduction in which Laurie recalls her initial interview with the principal? He stresses that "her job is to teach these kids to respect their country and to grow up to be good citizens." The community, he tells her, "expect us to mold these kids, to teach them proper behavior and respect for authority . . .." He concludes by reminding her that she has "the chance to teach them about our forefathers, and the Constitution, and about the wars we have won . . .." Let us examine the principal's assumptions, for taken as a whole, they are completely consistent and make perfect sense. Let us look at the key term, "citizenship."

In this dialogue, the principal reflects what we have designed as "Citizenship Transmission." The essential term is "citizenship." The social studies teacher's job, the principal insists, is to create "good citizens." But please note, "good citizenship" is defined by right knowledge, "proper behavior," and "respect for authority." Now, note, also, that Laurie is encouraged to generate loyalties, values, and attitudes by studying about "our forefathers, and the Constitution, and about the wars we have won . . .."

The term "Citizenship Transmission" refers to a mode of teaching in which the teachers intend that certain behaviors, knowledge, outlooks, and values will be learned by their students. These behaviors, knowledge, etc., are traditional in the culture in which both teacher and student participate. The teacher is literally *transmitting* those extremely important cultural patterns which he believes society wishes him to transmit.

The end or purpose of this tradition, as the name suggests, is citizenship. However, the term "citizenship" must be defined precisely as it is meant by Citizenship Transmitters. A citizen is one who conforms to certain accepted practices, holds particular beliefs, is loyal to certain values, participates in certain activities, and conforms to norms which are often local in character. Two authors[3] succinctly and accurately summarize the purpose of citizenship transmission in their explanation to students of the meaning of "good citizenship."

> A good citizen is the citizen who carries out all of the duties and responsibilities of American citizenship. Good citizenship means that the citizen is a good member of the American nation. Good citizenship means that the citizen obeys the laws, pays his taxes, and attends school . . . Good citizenship means that he is willing to help defend his country.

The emphasis in this definition is on *participation*. Knowing what is expected of him, the good citizen fulfills those expectations. This definition also emphasizes *acceptance*. This means simply that one has internalized certain norms. Without being especially conscious of doing so, the person -- the im-

21

mature person, the child -- quietly and slowly has incorporated a set of attitudes, values, and convictions. Some of these outlooks are derived from the entire society; that is, they are national in scope. These include paying taxes, attending schools, and defending one's country. Some of the norms and beliefs -- in fact, we believe, most of them -- reflect local norms. That is, they are beliefs about what is considered desirable moral behavior held by inhabitants of a particular region.

For instance, teachers commonly believe that they must, that they have absolutely no choice except to teach what the community expects them to teach. Despite the unconstitutionality and illegality of teacher's leading students in prayer in the public schools, many teachers assert that they would obey the community if it insisted that they lead prayers. By the same token, if citizens in the community hold that labor unions are noble and humane institutions which must be protected and preserved, teachers would be most willing to teach this belief. If the prevailing regional conviction is that Blacks are inferior, teachers would transmit this conviction. If, on the other hand, the dominant local belief is that Blacks have a place in the sun and that integration is desirable, then teachers would be perfectly willing to convey this view.

The social studies teacher as transmitter, according to our definition of purpose, is one who has accepted a particular belief, whatever it may be. He believes and his behavior reflects his belief. He would wish that his students behave and feel similarly. In short, the teacher defines a good citizen as one who holds certain values and attitudes, conforms to accepted practices, and participates in the accepted civic procedures.

One point must be emphasized. Transmission does not refer only to transmission of mainline, traditional values. Transmitters are by no means necessarily conservative. Whether it is teachers at Freedom Schools, radicals at some alternative schools, members of the John Birch Society or adherents of any other philosophical position, a teacher can be labeled "transmitter" if he teaches in such a way that he intends for students to emerge holding certain beliefs, values, and convictions. Transmission, then, does not refer to a particular *value* that is transmitted but rather to a particular *intention*.

22

If the intention of the Citizenship Transmitter is to bring about belief in and allegiance to a set of values which he believes are essential to the preservation of society, what is the purpose of those whom we designate as advocates of Social Studies taught as the Social Sciences?

Purpose as Conceived by the Social Science Position

Once again, we ask you to recall some dialogue from our introduction. Do you remember the impassioned speech of Arthur Leonard, the bright young anthropologist who wishes to convert Laurie? He tells her that his course is "based on the assumption that students can learn to think critically by observing the inquiry process of social scientists." The Arapesh, he advocates, are to be studied so that students can learn firsthand "how primitive society works; how people live, how they raise children." The young are to learn anthropology "by doing many of the same things real anthropologists do." He concludes by insisting that "the best way to train youth effectively is to teach them to think scientifically."

Although there are many variations on the Social Science position, we can say that the purpose is to create *future citizens* who have thoroughly learned the way of thinking of social scientists.[4] This way of thinking, it is held, has been fruitful in yielding perceptive, discriminating researchers who know how to interpret and use social knowledge. To the extent that young people learn this way of thinking, they, too can be equally perceptive and discriminating.

The interpretation of the term "citizenship" by advocates of the Social Science position is far more complex than the other two traditions. As we have seen, the transmitter equates citizenship with the internalization of certain beliefs and loyalties, with proper participation, and with correct attitudes. The Social Scientist would consider such a position to be parochial and indoctrinative. In all likelihood, the Social Scientist would draw from the lengthy history of the liberal arts for his definition of citizenship. When a Social Scientist says that his teaching method will yield good citizens, what he means is that the student should have learned a mode of thinking from social science disciplines; that this mode of thinking is generalizable;

23

and that having learned it, he will understand properly, appreciate deeply, infer carefully, and conclude logically. In effect, the Social Scientist means pretty much what his liberal arts colleagues in the past have always meant by the phrase "liberating the mind."

This mode of thinking, as we have seen, centers around the structure of the discipline which is also defined as a process, that is, a process by which scholars come to know. One component of this process consists of the large, overarching generalizations found within each discipline. For instance, the discipline of economics includes one familiar generalization with which you are acquainted: it is that man has unlimited wants but nature provides only limited resources. The discipline known as anthropology contains its important generalizations, which, taken collectively, form an intellectual structure. One such generalization is that there are certain universal ways of behaving, called cultural universals, which are to be found, with infinite variations, in all societies. All disciplines include generalizations which are extremely important. Whether called principles, axioms or assumptions, these major generalizations define the concerns and interests of each discipline.

In addition to important generalizations, the term structure also refers to the process by which scholars within a particular discipline gain new knowledge. Each discipline includes certain knowledge-gaining techniques which enable researchers to acquire and to verify their hypotheses. The archaeologist digs in the ground or under the ocean to unearth artifacts; he subjects them to a variety of testing and analytical procedures; and he attempts to make inferences about the culture from which the artifacts were derived. The sociologist interviews individuals, sends out questionnaires, and attempts to see how well his data fit his original hypothesis. The historian delves into archives, collects and often translates documents, and attempts to weave a pattern of events by which he can reconstruct the past. Each of these examples illustrates the meaning of the term "the process by which new knowledge is gained."

As they slowly gain insight and use the structure of the discipline, students are encouraged to acquire the thinking patterns of social science disciplines. Students are then in a

24

position to use these same thinking patterns later in their own lives as they come to grapple with the problems that inevitably arise in a political democracy.

In brief, proponents of the social science position hold that the purpose is to produce citizens who have learned the thinking patterns of social scientists. That is, they perceive the world as social scientists perceive it and they use the social scientist's conceptual framework in making decisions. It has followed that the social scientists' task is defined as teaching a new generation of social studies teachers the intricate and subtle modes of hypothesizing, gathering data, making references, and reaching conclusions employed by the various social science disciplines.

In sum, those who advocate the teaching of the social studies as social science believe that the best preparation for citizenship in a democracy is training in the modes of thinking employed by social scientists. Students who learn to think about complex issues with the skill and precision of social scientists are best able to analyze the workings, structure, and problems of the society which they will soon inherit.

Now, what of the approach of those whom we designate Reflective Inquirers?

Purpose as Conceived by Reflective Inquirers

The authors have made Kathy Wilhelm, Connie Goodrich, and Dr. Myers spokesmen for the position we call "Social Studies Taught as Reflective Inquiry." Recall, for a moment, Mrs. Wilhelm's argument with another teacher. She admits that DeeDee is a very attractive girl, "but it is possible to reach her, once you get her interested in something . . .." Connie Goodrich takes a similar position. She defends her teaching by saying, "What could possibly be more worthwhile than to help the kids gain an understanding of their own values?" And later, "I really try to get my students involved in the controversies that surround us. I want them to think for themselves." And the path to this goal is to "help the kids think critically about the issues of the day."

The key words here are "interests," "values," "critical

thinking" and "becoming involved in controversies that surround us." The Reflective Inquiry position is built upon a very few assumptions -- assumptions which run contrary to almost everything believed by Citizenship Transmitters. And, even though our Reflective Inquiry advocates use some of the same words as Social Scientists, they really are not tuned in to the same frequency.

The ultimate aim of advocates of this position is citizenship. But citizenship to Reflective Inquirers means something quite different than citizenship as defined by those whom we have described as Citizenship Transmitters and Social Science advocates. As defined by Reflective Inquirers, citizenship refers to the process of making rational, considered, well thought-out decisions.

The rationale for this definition -- which we will expand on in Chapter IV -- is that those who live in this society are continually caught in complex situations which require them to make decisions in morally ambiguous circumstances.

This definition of "citizenship" is inextricably related to the characteristics of this society and we ought now therefore say a few words about our society. Its most prominent characteristic is that it is a political democracy. "Democracy" is a complex term not capable of a short definition, but all agree that what makes a democracy distinctive is that those who are governed must govern themselves. That is, in some fashion the people make the basic regulations, the ground plans, by which they agree to be ruled. Second, because of the extremely rapid advance of technology, the spread of communication and the ease of transportation, very rapid social change -- in our democracy at any rate -- is the norm. The swiftness of social change has meant that attitudes, beliefs, and values are constantly in the process of being altered, shifted, and modified. Third, we are a diverse, pluralistic society. This means simply that our society consists of a variety of races, religious, regional outlooks, economic theories, philosophies, and social beliefs.

The social reality, then, is that individuals at any age are called upon to make decisions in a complex, rapidly changing social order in which value conflict is the rule rather than the exception. Inquiry teachers believe that decisions are not postponed until "later" but begin when one is confronted by choice. It follows that the process of inquiry should be taught when one enters kindergarten and continues through the rest of one's life.

Reflective Inquirers formulated their position in large part as a reaction to the Transmission tradition. As you will recall, the Citizenship Transmitter believes that there are certain values and items of knowledge which it is his duty to transmit to the young. To the extent that the young acquire the "correct" knowledge and values, they will become good citizens. Reflective Inquirers define this as an attempt to inculcate children to preconceived cultural norms of what is good and true. Given the extraordinary variations with regard to notions of goodness and truth, those who think that they are only translating what the "community" or "society" wants them to teach are -- in the eyes of the Reflective Inquirers -- simply kidding themselves. In reality, they are transmitting a selected, particularistic outlook.

What then do Reflective Inquirers think about values and how do they handle the question of what knowledge to teach? Rather than indoctrinating a particular set of social values, Reflective Inquiry advocates believe that it is essential for students to engage *in a continual process of clarifying their own value structure.* Inquirers believe that it is not *given* in advance that a particular value, belief, social position, or philosophy is better than another. Nor does it follow in fact or logic that a particular economic theory must be accorded loyalty. Nor is a particular conception of racial relations known to be good in advance, awaiting only transmission to students. This position, based upon diversity and cultural pluralism, is that each individual's distinctive task is to make a rational selection among all competing positions.

With regard to knowledge, two concepts seem to be essential to this tradition. First, Reflective Inquirers do not separate the *knowing* from the *valuing* process. Facts are not split off in a realm distinct and separate from values. The Reflective Inquiry advocate believes that the process of clarifying values involves knowledge. As an individual attempts to decide for himself what is desirable, he must obtain knowledge, information, data, and facts. One does not make decisions nor does one come to value without needing and using facts. Second, to the question,

27

What Knowledge ought people have? the Reflective Inquirer answer, That knowledge which people use.

The hooker in this sentence is, of course, "use." What is meant by "use?" The Reflective Inquirer believes that knowledge is used when individuals attempt to deal with some interest, concern, problem or need. As individuals faced with ambiguous circumstances try to figure out what they ought to feel, believe, or do, they *use* knowledge. That is, they employ knowledge as *data*. That knowledge necessary to have, then, is what the individual must acquire in order to act in his own best self-interest. Or, to put it another way, valid knowledge is what an individual needs in order to become an autonomous decision-maker.

The assumption is that the process of value clarification and knowledge acquisition -- and, to repeat, the two processes are not separable -- is the skill Reflective Inquirers wish to teach in order to create autonomous decision-makers who can function in a political democracy.

Conclusion

If the reader is -- quite understandably -- thinking, "That's nice. So there are three traditions within the social studies. What does this mean to me? How is it supposed to help me become an effective social studies teacher?" We should like to conclude with a restatement of our original introduction.

Assume for the moment that one's theoretical understanding of the social studies functions like a map.[5] Now, also assume that just as a map tells one what a particular terrain is like and how one might negotiate that terrain, the way one thinks about the social studies, similarly, provides direction. How one thinks about the social studies tells one what content to select, how to treat it, how to evaluate learning, what values are important and how "success" in teaching is to be defined.

The problem is that social studies teachers throughout this century have been operating with a faulty map -- or perhaps more accurately, with different maps --- which, in effect, has told drivers to head in several directions at once. Year after year, teachers have been told that they:

must make children into loyal citizens

must teach patriotism, respect for the law, and obedience to
authorities

should draw their curriculum content from the social sciences

should respect their students' views, whatever they may be

are responsible for socializing the young to the end that they
get along well with everyone

must lead children into a modern society, and that this
process requires learning a more appropriate set of
values and beliefs

One can take two views of this list. One can believe, "Yes,
that's right, we ought to do all of these things." Or one can conclude that these objectives are so inherently inconsistent that
there is no possibility that a teacher can realize all of them.

The authors take the second point of view. To try to teach
young people that they ought to hold all of the "right" beliefs
and that they should learn to critically examine all points of view
is to ask for the impossible. To respect students' views is one
thing; to replace them with another "more appropriate" set is
something else. To attempt to do both is to condemn the
teacher to a life of frustration, indecisiveness, inconsistency, and
ineffectiveness. To those who would operate with a clear map
we suggest, "Learn to identify and to evaluate the different
positions that are held by social studies teachers."

We conclude, finally, by one last return to our inquiry social
studies teacher, Laurie Townsley, who, as you may recall, does
not know what to say when a couple of brash high school kids
ask her, "What *kind* of social studies do you teach?" Laurie
feels called upon to make a decision, to commit herself to a way
of looking at the social studies. Unfortunately for Laurie -- and
everyone else -- *how* she is to decide is disturbingly elusive.
Laurie, can, of course, simply go with the most attractive person
in the teacher's lounge. She can for instance become like Art
Leonard because he is smart, well trained, and nice -- not to
mention good-looking. However, this is basically an irrational
way of choosing.

What Laurie ought to do is to learn how to listen to those
teachers. First, she ought to assume that what any teacher says

should be understood within a context, within a frame of reference. Second, she might -- from our standpoint -- assume that the way to understand the principal's desire for good behavior or a teacher's concern for interests is to interpret such behavior within a larger set of meanings. This is how our entire Three Traditions hypothesis functions: as a way of looking at teaching such that you see not only what teachers say but what they indeed mean to convey and what consequences flow from their beliefs.

One last word to students -- in particular, to some imagined detractors who mutter, "I just don't want to be labeled. Don't pin a label on me." Granted, your desire for uniqueness, for individuality. Granted, too, that labels are not always and forever accurate. However, we argue that teachers do tend to behave in predictable and repeated patterns. What we have done is to name some of these predictable and repeated patterns. We therefore entreat you not to protest against the terms, but to ask whether the terms do indeed describe real teaching behavior. And then we request that you ask yourself what kind of behavior you feel you can live with.

A Word About the Organization

The purpose of the introduction, essentially a case study, is to acquaint readers with problems of the social studies as they occur in an everyday setting. The purpose of Chapter I, which you have just finished reading, is to lay out the themes of this book. We wish to suggest that Laurie, you, and all other social studies teachers, should begin to think about the social studies in a certain way, using certain conceptual categories.

In Chapters II, III and IV, we are going to develop these categories by spelling out the meaning, origins, significance, and consequences of what we see as three historical traditions within the social studies. In no sense are these new traditions. They can be seen from the beginning of recorded history, from the time Plato described Socrates' questioning style, and from the period in which the ancient rabbis trained their students in the Sacred Scripture. We call these three traditions "Social Studies Taught as Citizenship Transmission," "Social Studies Taught as the Social Sciences" and "Social Studies Taught as Reflective

Inquiry." To abbreviate these admittedly clumsy terms, we call them Transmission, Social Science, and Reflective Inquiry.

Chapters II, III and IV are organized around three questions or categories. We selected this form of organization because it reflects the actual questions that each teacher asks and answers. These questions are, first, What is the purpose of social studies?, second, What is the method of social studies? and third, How does one select content? The first question can be reduced to one idea. For what reasons is social studies taught? or, phrased differently, What is the most important outcome that I want as a result of students having taken my course? The second question means roughly, How would I, as a teacher, go about organizing ideas and teaching them to students? That is, What principles or generalizations guide me as I decide how to teach? Finally, the third question, How does one select content? can be translated to mean, Now that I know *why* I am teaching and *how* it is to be done, with what content am I going to do it?

There is a final section, Chapter V, which is both a wrap-up and way of checking yourself out. This chapter contains a self-check test which you might wish to take and which is designed to tell you where you probably fit in terms of these three traditions.[6] Following the self-check test is an analysis of the three different patterns of answers and what they signify in terms of the three traditions thesis.

The intended audience for this work is primarily, but not exclusively, those who are either preparing for a career in social studies or for those who already teach in the field. We feel, however, that professors of social studies, educational foundations and curriculum, might also benefit from a reading of this book. Our purpose in writing this work is not persuasion but rather the desire to enable teachers of the social studies to become more discriminating and more intelligent in their approach. And, we believe, in becoming more reflective, teachers will become more competent.

[1] James L. Barth and S. Samuel Shermis, "Defining the Social Studies: An exploration of Three Traditions," *Social Education,* 37 No. 7 (November,1970) 743-751.

[2] For the past 70 years there have been numerous attempts to define the social studies. Some of the more significant contemporary contributors to that attempt are: Edgar Bruce Wesley, *Teaching the Social Studies, op. cit.;* Shirley H. Engle, "Objectives of the Social Studies," *New Challenges in the Social Studies,* Byron G. Massialas and Frederick R. Smith, editors (Belmont, California: Wadsworth Publishing Co., 1965); John Jarolimek, *Guidelines for Elementary Social Studies* (Washington, D.C.: Association for Supervision and Curriculum Development, 1967); James P. Shaver, "Social Studies: The Need for Redefinition," *Social Education,* 31 (November, 1967) 588; Dale L. Brubaker, *Alternative Directions for the Social Studies,* (Scranton, Pa.: International Textbook Co., 1967).

[3] William S. Hartley and William Vincent, *American Civics* (New York: Harcourt, Brace and World, 1967), p. 38.

[4] A fairly complete list and description of the various social studies projects can be found in *Social Education,* 36 (November, 1972).

[5] The map analogy is to be found in S. I. Hayakawa, *Language in Thought and Action* (New York: Harcourt, Brace Jovanavich, 1972, Third edition). Note that theory so defined is markedly different from theory defined as a set of hazy abstractions of no practical use in the "real" world. Theory as we tend to use the term is that which serves as a guide in the direction of the day-to-day activities.

[6] Readers wishing to know more about the origin, development, and statistical rationale of this self-check test, may obtain information by writing Professor James L. Barth, Social Studies Education, Education Building, Purdue University, West Lafayette, Indiana 47907.

CHAPTER II

Social Studies Taught As Citizenship Transmissions

The light came on and the students blinked their eyes against the sudden glare; some yawned or stretched, others turned to talk to an another. The film had been an engrossing documentary about Nazi brutality toward Jews during World War II. The teacher watched the last bit of film run through the projector and then switched off the machine. He stood quietly for a moment and then spoke to his class in a hushed, emotion charged voice; the class immediately turned toward their teacher and silence quickly spread throughout the room.

"You know," he said, " it has been written that he who forgets the past is doomed to repeat it." He then paused for a moment as if to reflect on his own words. No one in the class moved. He spoke again slowly, as if weighing each word, "We must never let such a thing happen again. There is nothing so precious as a human life...and yet our history has been a steady procession of man's inhumanity to man. Wars, rapes and murders, assassinations and concentration camps, slavery and persecutions...How can it be? Such suffering, such heartache, such sorrow." He paused again and then continued. "Look at our own country, the Charlie Mansons, and the Lt. Calleys, and the assassinations of the Kennedys and Martin Luther King. The shooting of George Wallace and the Olympic murders and Napalm and Nuclear bombs and..." Shaking his head, he is unable to continue. He then looks up at his students and slowly turns to gaze around the room. "We must put an end to this senseless waste," he said as his voice raised, "we must respect the dignity and worth of each individual in our society and even the world. Any less will doom us all to a rendezvous with disaster and destruction."

The teacher in this classroom episode is deeply involved in transmitting values to his students. He is using films, persuasion, and personal commitment to try to instill within young people what he considers to be basic values. He may see the transmission of these values as the primary and overriding educational outcome of his instructional process and work enthusiastically to insure that his goals are accomplished. In this, he is practicing what we have called "Citizenship Transmission."

Concern Over Value Relativity

Citizenship Transmission is perhaps the most widespread, accepted classroom approach to social studies teaching. Its proponents consider the instructional goals associated with this point of view to be not only vitally important to the body politic but to the survival of the race. As Joseph Junel has said, "The world of pure intelligence too easily condones the Auschewitz horror chambers and the charnel house of Hiroshima." He goes on to say, "We had better start telling them [students] what social goodness means and what are some of its great motivating forces. [One such force] is human worth. To this I would add such others as dignity, equality, compassion, and a few of the democratic freedoms."[1] To proponents of citizenship transmission, such value-laden ideas become the primary, all important instructional goals of the social studies.

The task of identifying the basic values of our culture and transmitting them to school youth, while always generating impressive support among social studies teachers, has, in recent years, taken on even more dynamic dimensions. Some argue that the widespread diversity and pluralism of our country demands that all American youth develop a basic set of unifying values and what is needed is some unifying cultural "togetherness." They fear that the trend toward objectivity and moral aloofness serves only to cause our society to degenerate into ethical relativism. In recent years an impressive array of scholars have begun to wonder out loud and in print what is happening to our nation. Why do so many people feel isolated, pointless, and even helpless? Why is there so much violence and corruption in our national life? In response to such anguished questions, Irving Kristol recently concluded at a Rockefeller

34

Foundation Symposium, "I think we can all agree that the United States and western civilization in general are experiencing what we call a crisis in values." At the same symposium, Paul Freund agreed and carried the idea to a logical conclusion. "It seems to me," he said, "that whatever you call them...values or virtue, or fundamentals...there is a considerable thirst among ordinary people for some mooring..." It is out of such an understandable concern for basic values that pressure is brought to bear on school social studies programs to provide our youth with just such a mooring.

The dangers of the ethical relativism of our contemporary age seem increasingly apparent. It has seemed that everyone from the National Soap-Box Derby winner to the President of the United States has exhibited a tendency toward amoral and unprincipled behavior. It exists in the Watergate break-in and cover-ups, the My Lai Massacre, and in government wiretapping, burglary, and perjury by high government officials. It is seen in Pentagon officials refusing to inform the American people of bombing raids in Cambodia and Laos and in the HEW Birth Control Clinics sterilization of young black girls. We have conceptualized and legitimatized this process by calling it a "credibility gap," and tragically we have come not only to accept it but to expect it. Jack Anderson, columnist for the *Washington Post,* put it like this:

> "Our belief in ourselves is unraveling under the stresses of shattering scandals, breakdowns and breaches of faith in high places. A sense of things gone wrong pervade the land, of values lost, of anger against those who symbolize that loss.
>
> "Whatever it was we were trying to do together, whatever it was we once stood for, is dissolving into uncertainty and disillusion...What is our national purpose? What is the source of our partiotism?"[2]

Anderson goes on to wonder what holds all of our diverse nationalities and sub-cultures together. His conclusion strongly emphasizes the citizenship transmission position:

> "What could possibly unite and give purpose to such a kaleidoscopic populace? Abraham Lincoln had an an-

35

swer: common belief in the ideas on which the nation was founded...There are many signs today of a hunger in the land for old truths. The time is at hand to turn this inchoate yearning into a movement of national regeneration."[3]

Many social studies teachers not only would agree with Jack Anderson, but would even go so far as to see themselves as the social agents directly responsible for teaching the younger generation the beliefs and values deemed necessary for good citizenship. The beliefs may consist of the highest ideals of the culture (all men are created equal; the worth and dignity of human life), certain patterns of behavior believed to be inherent in a democracy (obeying laws, voting, paying taxes), and certain class values (puritan ethic, respect for authority and honesty).

During recent years this concern has been seen in what the media refer to as the Back To Basics Movement. This movement has gathered momentum since a violent conflict erupted in Kanawha County in West Virginia where some parents objected to classroom instructional material dealing with sex, drugs, and violence. It has spread to include a growing number of parents throughout the country who are insisting that school return to classrooms where discipline, the three Rs, and the direct teaching of patriotism are stressed. Some school districts, like Pasadena, California, have responded by creating alternative Fundamental Schools that emphasize the "basics" and are available to parents on a voluntary basis.

The What and How Transmission

In order to obtain such desired outcomes, citizenship transmission teachers carefully select instructional content; but even more important, teachers interpret content for the students so that they will know what to conclude and how to feel about it. Thus a teacher might choose to study the New Deal in order to demonstrate the dangers of the welfare state; or Nazi Germany in order to show the dangers of authoritarian rule; or drugs in order to help help students learn the dangers in drug abuse. In each case, the specific content information is only of incidental value and may even be soon forgotten. What is of primary im-

36

portance is the basic generalizations, feelings, beliefs, and values that students gain from the content. Being older and wiser than the students, the teacher must be considered the authority and this enables him to instill those beliefs that are, he perceives, deemed important by society.

Not only does the teacher select content, he may even omit or slant information that does not support the desired learning outcome. Thus teachers may study Manifest Destiny, yet ignore the slaughter of Indians; may study the horrors of Nazi Germany, yet omit mention of Japanese relocation centers; or in their efforts to glorify the nation's past, simply overlook the Grant or Harding Administrations, and glance only slightly at the Spanish American War. The overriding instructional goal is not so much that the students remember the content but that content conveys a particular feeling or value that will hopefully survive long after information, fact, and detail are forgotten.

Thus, within a few months after taking American history, students will most likely have forgotten the details of all the wars and battle campaigns that were so carefully memorized for tests.
Yet, they will carry with them the feeling that America has won all its wars and that good people do not strike the first blow but always emerge victorious. One month after the American civics class, most students likely will not be able to recall the details of how a bill becomes a law, whether the State Superintendent of Education is appointed or elected, or the precise structure of the court system. What they will remember, however, is that our socio-political system -- abbreviated "our way of life" -- is the fairest and best ever devised by man and that, while it is not perfect, all problems will gradually be solved so that present inquities will disappear. Despite the enormous emphasis on memorization of discrete information, the eventual forgetting is not regarded as particularly regrettable. For the details themselves are secondary. It is the accompanying feeling, the underlying attitudes and values, that are designed to be transmitted.

Historical Development

Citizenship Transmission as an established learning goal is easily the oldest social studies position and in terms of an enduring impact on school programs and the teachers who people these programs, it is in a league all its own. Long before the term "social studies" or "reflective inquiry" had been coined or even before the development of the social science disciplines, teachers were diligently engaged in the task of transmitting to each new generation of Americans the knowledge which they believed would instill the positive patriotic principles essential for "good citizenship." And since "good citizenship" was felt to be intimately related to both the survival of the republic and the participation of each child in the "good life," this goal was not taken lightly. If achieving the goal of public schools -- i.e, "good citizenship" -- meant that certain "unpleasant" facts would have to be omitted and that certain men and situations viewed only in a favorable light, such could be justified by the meritorious goal to which the activities were dedicated. Since the 1880's teachers have been charged repeatedly by national commissions and committees to teach their students good citizenship and to approach their task of "citizenship education" with vigor; to drill their students again and again on "essential" information -- names, dates, events, and places; and if their students forgot them, to teach them again.[4] For, as we have said, not only was information considered important, it was even more essential for "molding" the proper values and beliefs of school youth.

The Origins of Transmission

Such educational practices are certainly not new or confined to this society. Some would argue the practice of cultural transmission is as old as man himself. This is certainly not an indefensible claim. Ancient literature is full of examples of the use of stylized stories of the past to teach the wisdom, ideals, and values of the culture. Such works as the Homeric Epics, the Hebrew Sacred Scripture, and the New Testament are crowded with heroic tales and moral parables designed to inspire youth to value and to attain the high ideals handed down through the ages. Such works as these also served as the primary educational material for youth. The content and treatment parallel in many ways the concept that would later turn up as citizenship transmission.

38

But the practices associated with citizenship transmission probably extend even beyond great epic literature of the past. We can only speculate that it found its beginning in the simple desire of the elders of the family or tribe to pass on to the young the ideals and understandings that had served them well. Thus, cultural transmission was a survival strategy of the tribe. The practice of using mythical tales of past heroes to teach cultural ideals probably developed out of the habit of story-telling around the campfires. Through such stories, children learned their cultural identity, the ideals and values of the group, and most especially models for behavior. While such practices can be traced back into history and pre-history, they can be seen in the techniques of child rearing practiced by families in contemporary societies.

As early man became more sophisticated, cultural transmission was institutionalized. It proved to be a forerunner of literature, gave impetus to the development of history as a discipline, and even became the primary goal of formal education. Since the time of Plato, education has consisted of passing on -- transmitting -- the accumulated knowledge of preceeding generations to each new generation. And, since it has always been assumed that each new generation would live substantially the same as the one that preceeded it, the role of education was seen as transmitting the knowledge and understanding necessary for what had always been assumed to be the "good life." Until very recently this educational goal was unquestioned. As long as society was changing slowly and the accumulated wisdom of mankind was small, it may have been possible for schools to transmit the essential, necessary knowledge; and if the effectiveness of this educational goal is open to question now, one thing is fairly certain: schools did in fact choose cultural transmission as the primary objective of their teaching.

Some educators have argued that each new generation redefines the role of education and articulates new goals for teaching. In the case of citizenship transmission, that is certainly not true. Since 1892, when the NEA Committee of Ten formally recommended "good citizenship" as the appropriate end of public education, social studies as citizenship transmission has exhibited both a powerful influence and a tenacious durability. For the better part of 80 years, "citizenship transmission" has been almost synonymous with social studies education; at least as it was practiced in our nation's schools."[5] The persuasiveness of this theory of social studies is still clearly apparent; it is alive and well and functioning in an unusually large number of our nation's schools even today. Preserved by state laws, nationalistic pressures, and the unquestioned conviction that students can be taught to become patriotic citizens, social studies as citizenship transmission has pervaded the formal education of our nation's youth and withstood almost every effort to dislodge it, revise it, or even dampen the belief in its promised effect.

Cultural Diversity and Transmission Techniques

While social studies as citizenship transmission is associated with idealistic, humanitarian values, in practice it is often identified in simplistic and largely negative terms of overt indoctrination through the use of gross propaganda. George Washington "never told a lie," Lincoln was scrupulously honest; the U.S. never started nor lost a war; police are usually characterized as "community helpers"; soldiers are usually designated as "national heroes", and fair play and sportsmanship are "the American way." There are also other rather dramatic illustrations from fairly recent textbooks. The following passage was taken from William H. Hartley and William S. Vincent, *American Civics:*

> If the United States is to continue to be the greatest nation in the world, we cannot sit back and relax our efforts. We must work harder to improve our free enterprise system better than ever. We must prove that capitalism can bring ever-greater benefits to all our citizens and at the same time make our nation's economy grow and prosper.[6]

Another recent book provides a similar illustration:

> The United States today is the richest and most powerful nation in the history of the world. People in this country have a kind of freedom enjoyed by very few other

40

peoples, either past or present. They can criticize the government openly, in speeches or books or magazines or newspaper. And the government pays attention to what is said.[7]

In the hands of a dedicated teacher, such textbook passages can become unquestioned principles and are in practice used in conjunction with vast numbers numbers of cues and conditioning to encourage the students toward the instructional goal, i.e., internalizing the "right" values and attitudes. So subtle is much of the "enculturalization" of basic values and ideals that it has been referred to as the "hidden curriculum.[8] Everything in schools, the flag, classroom decorations and pictures, the dress and language of the teacher, and the behavioral rules of the classroom can reflect citizenship transmission goals. For example, consider the following illustration:

Scattered memorabilia of the nation's past clutter the classroom; Americana is everywhere. George Washington and Abraham Lincoln face each other from opposite ends of the room, and the boredom of the class is reflected in their vacant stares. The U.S. flag and the Ohio state flag frame the chalk-board like a stage. Inspirational mottoes and quotations, carefully handprinted by extra-credit-hungry students hang here and there proclaiming such things as "Know Thyself," "I Am What I Know," "Give Me Liberty Or Give Me Death," "Ask Not What Your Country Can Do For You..." and a variety of other catchy comments. The Constitution and the Declaration of Independence, chemically yellowed to dramatize the aged reverence of the documents, are pinned to the bulletin board, prepared and presented by the local chapter of the D.A.R. Lincoln's Gettysburg Address is also there, and Wilson's 14 Points. On a bookshelf sits a chalk statuette of U.S. Grant and an inaccurate replication of John F. Kennedy in pseudobronze. There are also charts explaining "How a Bill Becomes Law," the "Separation of Powers," and an organizational outline of the local municipal government. The middle-age teacher sits facing his class of fifth graders neatly seated in perfectly straight rows. He is talking to the students about their responsibilities as citizens. "In a few years," he says, "each of you will be 18 years of age, and you will have the opportunity to participate in free elections of this country. But it is so much more than an opportunity, it is in fact, your national responsibility. In order to keep our country strong," his voice rising to emphasize his challenge, "you must be informed on the issues and know the candidate's position on the issues and vote for the man of your choice." This last phrase was stamped out in stacatto fashion, with each word and each syllable emphasized by the vigorous throbbing of his open hand against the desk.

Rising from his desk he continues, "But voting is only one of your responsibilities. Let's turn in our books to page 32, and look at what our text has to say about this issue." The teacher opens his book to a section entitled, "What the Good Citizen Does" and asks for volunteers to read the passage. Several hands go up and the teacher calls on a girl in the front row. "Laura, now sit up straight and talk loud enough for everyone to hear, and read for us the eight responsibilities listed here." She wiggles to a tense upright position and reads the list in a loud voice: "(1) Votes intelligently, (2) Keeps well informed, (3) Helps create public opinion, (4) Pays taxes, (5) Serves in public office, (6) Performs military service, (7) Serves on juries, (8) Works in political parties."

That's very good, Laura, I hope all of you will think about each of those things very carefully, for they are the primary things I want you to learn during this course. You should learn this list not just remember them, but to help you think about your personal duty to your country. In this way you will surely become a better citizen and in turn our great country will become even stronger.

Illustrations of such obvious efforts at citizenship transmissions are easy to come by but often fail to adequately depict the subtleties and complexities of the point of view. If our culture were homogenous or if there were agreement on the right values to inculcate, the position would be intelligible. Unfortunately, no such homogeniety exists. The most obvious characteristic of contemporary American culture is widespread conflict and controversy. Our culture is "shot through" with diversity and value conflict between and among groups, forced to co-exist and clashing continuously over goals. America is red, white, and black...and brown, bronze, and yellow. It is composed of Chinese and Chicanos, Indians and Irish, Jews and Gentiles, Africans and Armenians, not to mention French, British, Germans, Czechs, and on and on. A remarkable collection of the world's "tired...huddled masses" somehow held together by the slender thread of tolerance, tradition, and geographic proximity. America is a cultural collage of black and white, young and old, elite and alienated, the very rich and the very poor, Democrats and Republicans, rednecks and radicals. There are Black Panthers, Masons, John Birchers, Jesus Freaks, Weathermen, Junior Executives, Lions clubbers, S.D.S., New Left, Old Guard, and innumerable short and long-lived, informal and formal groups and gatherings. Americans speak many languages and worship many gods; and each sub-culture has its own unique histories and traditions, customs and tastes, and the values of each are often offensive to the other. To talk of cultural transmissions in the midst of such diversity immediately raises the problem of transmitting values.

Conflicting Ideals

A teacher might choose to transmit a wide variety of very different values, depending on his own personal beliefs, national and community ideals, or universal commitments.

1. *Universal Ideals:* At the entrance to the Indiana University School of Education, a quote by Caleb Mills is etched in limestone and says "Teachers Must Inspire As Well As Instruct." Many social studies teachers would read Mill's quote and agree totally and completely. They see their role as inspiring to attain "higher" ideals. One teacher recently confirmed to one of the authors his deep concern for his students. "They don't seem to believe in anything. Just a 'get-it-while-you-can' approach to life that seems completely devoid of any higher meaning." The teacher saw his role as trying to "instill

some appreciation for the more noble, enduring aspects of civilization." A similar effort at inspiring respect of universal ideals was described in the classroom illustrations that opened this chapter.

2. *National Ideals:* A teacher may also desire to transmit patriotic ideals and values associated with nationalism or the democratic philosophy. This certainly appears to be most common and is the classical case for teaching "Americanism." Most of the more obvious examples of citizenship transmission grow out of this particular point of view.

3. *Regional/Local Ideals:* One of the complicating factors involved in citizenship transmissions is that regional or local community ideals may differ dramatically with universal or national ideals. Teachers in Waycross, Georgia, New Trier, Illinois, Detroit, Michigan, and Berkeley, California, would find themselves surrounded by very different and very powerful community preassures. Thus teachers may be torn between beliefs that "all men are created equal" and local racial, religious, or ethnic biases, the belief in democratic procedures and the acceptance of local machine politics, a belief in a strong federal government, and the prevailing community fear of "creeping socialism." This is often the primary concern of new teachers. You will remember that even Socrates was asked to leave town for teaching youth ideals that differed from community norms.

Not long ago a social studies graduate who took a position in Jeffersonville, Indiana brought in the following newspaper story:

Transmission of U.S. Heritage in Peril

The United States is in danger today of failing to transmit its heritage, Dr. Kenneth McFarland, a nationally known lecturer on Americanism, said yesterday in a speech to a Southeast Division conference of the Indiana State Teachers Association of Jeffersonville. Dr. McFarland, who is a former teacher and school superintendent, said *that every child wants to be idealistic and must be taught that "nothings is more basically right than the fundamental American system."* He said the system rests on the framework of free enterprise and sovereignty of the individual, and the foundation of the frame is spiritual tradition. "The people who wrote the constitution read Biblical scripture and believed it," he said, "This can be legally taught under the Supreme Court rulings and must be if we are going to transmit the heritage." McFarland said that as a boy he met William Jennings Bryan, the noted political leader and orator at the turn of the century, who asked the young McFarland what he wanted to be. McFarland said he told Bryan, "I want to be like you and lift my voice to tell the glories of God and the United States of America." He said Bryand advised him "to go down on your knees every night and ask God to give you gumption and don't ever ask anything from anyone else." "He was transmitting the heritage," McFarland said of Bryan and he told the teachers that this also is "your job and your opportunity." The teachers gave him a standing ovation.[9]

After showing the news article, the young teacher commented, "I can't believe that stuff, but the other teachers were on their feet applauding that guy. I don't want to be a propaganda machine, but I also don't want to lose my job. I feel so lucky to have found a job and I'm not about to jeopardize it by bucking the other teachers and community."

4. *Pluralistic Cultural Ideals:* Further complicating the issue is the complex and often conflicting ideals and values found in our pluralistic culture. Blacks in inner-city schools may choose to transmit cultural values that stand in stark contrast to those of white middle-class teachers. They may attempt to inculcate in their students the sentiment that "Black is beautiful" and encourage political activism to the point of political resistance. Many new left, counter-culturists who have entered the classroom in free and alternative schools, while deploring indoctrination in public schools, often seem more doctrinaire in their beliefs than their "straight" counterparts in public education. Visits to a large number of "free schools" have revealed hip, avant-garde teachers addressing the students on the conformity, mediocrity, and inhuman institutional systems in this country. Often the teachers are earnestly trans-

45

mitting liberal sexual attitudes, endorsement of mind-expanding drugs, and a "return to the earth" rural mythology. And while their textbooks may be the Whole Earth Catalog or the writings of Carlos Castaneda, their approach to teaching is nearly identical to that of the public school teacher who transmits conventional values about the system.

5. *Personal Ideals and Values:* Since each person holds personal values, beliefs and ideals, teachers attempting citizenship transmission may find themselves confronted by a good deal of confusion. An individual's values are often inconsistent and ill-defined. One may incorporate into his own value system highly incongruent beliefs, or beliefs that are in opposition to national ideals or local community norms. A teacher may attempt to transmit highly personal values about sex, religion, marriage, dress, and drugs. He may also choose to transmit personal political views. This, of course, leads to a good deal of confusion on the part of the student whose teachers over the years may hold widely different personal values.

This brief survey of distinctly different and often conflicting perceptions of ideals suggest the range of values that could be transmitted and should help to clarify the wide variances in this approach to social studies education. It also should help to emphasize a number of inherent dilemmas in citizenship transmission.

Instructional Goals of Citizenship Transmission

While there are a wide variety of conflicting value positions that may be transmitted, the overriding purpose of citizenship transmission is usually associated with effective democratic citizenship. The instructional goals that are assumed to be necessary prerequisites to effective democratic citizenship are threefold. The students are to learn a body of "accepted" information about their heritage, a correct interpretation of the content, and from both what is usually assumed to be enduring values. The following statement from the National Council for Social Studies suggests the content of citizenship transmission:

Through civic education our youth are helped to gain
an understanding of our national ideals, the common

good, and the process of self-government. Similarly our youth are helped to comprehend the meaning -- both within the United States and throughout the world -- of freedom for themselves and all men, for the individual and for the group, in creed and commerce, in ballot and daily behavior. They are helped to understand the various civil liberties guaranteed in our Constitution and Bill of Rights and the accompanying civic responsibilities by which alone they can be achieved.[10]

Even more explicit relationships with citizenship transmissions are found in the following list of instructional goals taken from course syllabi and textbooks currently in use. They have been selected from a wide variety of different social studies courses and should help to illustrate the avowed goals of citizenship transmission:

1. Developing a reasoned patriotism.

2. Developing a basic understanding and appreciation of American values, institutions, and practices.

3. To inspire personal integrity and responsible citizenship.

4. To build an understanding and appreciation of the American heritage.

5. To encourage active democratic participation.

6. To help pupils acquire an awareness of social problems.

7. Developing and exhibiting desirable ideals, attitudes, and behavioral skills which are essential in good personal relations with others. The emphasis is on habitual desirable behavior, not mere appreciation of good or a desire to do what is right.

8. To understand and appreciate the free enterprise system.

In the late 1950's, the Committee on Concepts and Values of the National Council for the Social Studies identified 14 "themes" as societal goals of the American democracy. Each of these themes were felt by the committee to represent values held by the majority of Americans and as such were believed to encompass the basic instructional goals of value education. The themes were as follows:

1. The intelligent use of the forces of nature.

2. Recognition and understanding of world interdependence.

3. Recognition of the dignity and worth of the individual.

4. Use of intelligence to improve human living.

5. Vitalization of democracy through the intelligent use of our public educational facilities.

6. Intelligent acceptance, by individuals and groups, of responsibility for achieving democratic social action.

7. Increasing effectiveness of the family as a basic social institution.

8. Effective development of moral and spiritual values.

9. Intelligent and responsible sharing of power in order to attain justice.

10. Intelligent utilization of scarce resources to attain the widest general well-being.

11. Achievement of adequate horizons of loyalty.

12. Cooperation in the interest of peace and welfare.

13. Achieving balance between social stability and social change.

14. Widening and deepening the ability to live more richly.

In each of these statements the goals of citizenship transmission are clearly apparent. The students are to learn *about* their history, heritage, and the workings of the American government and economy. Clearly, there is a body of knowledge the student is expected to learn. The students are also to learn a particular interpretation of this body of knowledge. i.e., there is a right "understanding." But most important, the students learn a particular feeling, attitude; or value from the knowledge and the interpretation. The student is to learn to "appreciate." The combined package of knowledge, understanding, and appreciations are assumed to have a direct effect on behavior so that if the social studies teacher is successful, the student is believed to become a more effective citizen.

From this description of the goals of citizenship transmission it becomes evident that the teacher who employs this approach is directly concerned with both the *cognitive* and the *affective domain*. The teacher is not only interested in teaching a body of knowledge, he is also interested in teaching a set of beliefs. The teacher knows what needs to be learned, and how one should feel about what is learned. As we have suggested earlier, the teacher may teach information about the New Deal, interpret, this federal program as the beginnings of a "welfare state," and then instruct the students that this is a threat to states' rights and should be avoided. A Chicano teacher in south Texas may choose to teach migrant worker children about the free enterprise system. He may interpret this system as one of political "exploitation" and instruct the students it is wanting and in need of drastic change. In each of these examples, the teacher selects the content, interprets the content, and instructs the students on how they should feel about it. In all such situations, the citizenship transmission teacher believes that these beliefs and values are so important they are to be accepted without question.

Content of Citizenship Transmission

The citizenship transmission instructional goals of "good citizenship" have had a pervasive effect on the social studies programs of our nation's schools. Since it was assumed that an indispensable ingredient in preparing "good" citizens was *knowledge* and *appreciation* of our heritage, it became absolutely necessary for school youth to study American history and American government. So important was this assumption held to be, that every state in the nation has legislated the required study of American history, often at the 5th, 8th, and 11th grade.[11] After the end of the Korean War, when a number of U.S. P.O.W.'s elected to remain in the Communist lands, most states likewise passed laws requiring that all students study the U.S. Constitution and the American Government.[12] Sometimes the specifics of the history and government courses have been spelled out in detail and have become a kind of "authorized" content for social studies programs. This "authorized" content has been sanctioned by state legislators and state departments of education, established as requirements for high school graduation and college entrance, and has become institutionalized in textbooks and teacher certification programs.

This "authorized" content for social studies programs is remarkably similar throughout the nation. The program is predominantly history, usually taught chronologically, almost always "covering" accepted topics. The last systematic survey of school social studies programs concluded the curriculum had not changed significantly in over 25 years and that in courses like U.S. history and government a definite series of topics composed them.[13] Even in courses named Problems of Democracy, there is a list of agreed upon problems that almost invariably appear. These course topics have become so accepted that newer textbooks that have omitted or even shuffled or retitled sections have been opposed by various community groups. But the accepted content is certainly not simply a result of community pressure; many learned committees have carefully identified the exact content that composed our nation's heritage, going so far as to list the important people, events, and even dates that are to be learned.

What has always mystified educators is that a fairly significant body of research has demonstrated that the social studies content deemed so essential for "good" citizenship is rapidly forgotten. Some have estimated that no more than 10% of the social studies content is retained even by the best motivated students. The majority of information in forgotten quickly, usually within two weeks. This very fact has led educators to conclude that we must "teach the material over and over again until the cumulative effect becomes lasting and enduring.[14] Thus U.S. History is usually taught three times during the twelve years of public education. If so much is forgotten, why then do teachers work so hard to teach the content? How do they justify the fantastic amount of time and energy required for teaching students factual information? The answer, of course, lies in the affective area. The factual information is used as a vehicle to transmit proper beliefs, values, and ideals.

Not only does Social Studies as Citizenship Transmission have a designated content, it is also characterized by serious omissions and idealized distortions. It takes little more than a casual visit to most public school social studies classes to realize the world about which students are studying is quite different from the world in which they live. Not only is the controversial and the disturbing ignored and omitted, but often what is studied is an exaggerated, idealized view of America's past. In the past, textbook descriptions have often bordered on gross propaganda. This is certainly not always the case, but a growing body of descriptive research suggests that many social studies programs have tried to homogenize the rich diversity of our culture into a single tradition, a single story, a single idealized history. Likewise, few of the conflicts and controversies within our tradition are found; and a careful examination of even relatively recent textbooks will turn up serious distortions, omissions, inconsistencies, and overgeneralizations. While more recent social studies textbooks generally are more accurate, a textual analysis of texts in the early 1960's led a group of historians to conclude:

> It is evident that reputable and widely used textbooks commit errors of omission or commission in their treatment of these periods. The fruits of historical scholarship are neglected and single-strand interpretations are left unquestioned. This fault is strikingly evidenced when probably quite unconsciously textbooks are building wholly improbable stereotypes of, say, patriotic, unselfish Founding Fathers or of a god-like super-statesman, Abraham Lincoln. Discussion of old war tensions is conducted in terms of good guys and bad guys. The average high school student is often reading not the results of careful historical research and evaluation, but propaganda ... It is a grave charge to make, but the conclusion is inescapable; under this treatment our students' minds tend to be closed, not widened. Students whose history reading is largely confined to the textbook (and there are many such) are subjected to a brain-washing as complete as it is dangerous.[15]

Research since the late 1960's has also identified a variety of omissions from social studies courses. The history and culture of many ethnic minorities have been distorted, deleted, or simply omitted. This is true of Blacks, Chicanos, Native Americans, and women. Other studies have indicated social studies courses have tended to minimize the negative and unpleasant in American life. Such issues as racial injustice, crime, violence, poverty, class conflict, family disorganization, and the revolution in

51

sexual morals are usually ignored in social studies classes. In 1968 a similar study of both affluent suburban schools and urban slum schools revealed that both ignored the realities of poverty and class distinctions. The Report of the National Commission on the Causes and Prevention of Violence concluded that the violent nature of our country had often been hidden in school textbook images of America as the "Promised Land."

Student teachers who return to social studies classes to practice teach are often shocked and disturbed by what they find. One such teacher put it this way:

> They were not really studying history or culture or society, they were in fact studying a kind of mythology. While observing my cooperating teacher during the first few days and looking through the textbook, I began to get really scared.

Jonathon Kozol found a similar situation in the 1960's when he was teaching in the Boston Public Schools. He reported that at a time when the South was alive with freedom marchers, sit-ins, voter registration drives, cattle-prods, and violent clashes, a fellow teacher remarked, "Thank God, Johnnie, we can come to school and forget about all those terrible things in Alabama.[16]

What Lies Behind Transmission

But how can this be? Why would a profession dedicated to developing "good citizen" and helping students live more effectively in society condone such an unrealistic dichotomy between the classroom and the culture? Why is the curriculum predominatly a study of the past rather than the present or the future, and why is content so inconsistent with not only the academic disciplines but also the morning paper and the evening news?

Some have tried to explain these particular characteristics found in certain social studies classes as an unfortunate outgrowth of the "ignorance and timidity" of public school teachers. Others have argued that it is a simple case of "unconscious oversight." Some have explained it as proof of the inadequate preparation of teachers in the academic areas. And while these explanation may be partially correct, they are far too simplistic to completely explain such widespread practice and long-held beliefs. Far from being "unconscious," the practice of omitting and distorting course content or using the content to inculcate moral beliefs, seems to be a conscious effort to meet the desired ends of patriotic instruction. As such, the characteristics of certain school social studies programs that have been described are a logical extension of the goals of citizenship transmission.

One important note must also be made about the content of the citizenship transmission position. While it has been associated with some of the most inaccurate and distorted instructional materials and classroom lectures, it certainly is not limited to overt propaganda. Determined teachers often use the newest, inquiry-oriented materials to transmit values. The following classroom situation provides an illustration of this.

The class is located in a middle-class suburb of Houston, Texas in a new multi-million dollar high school of over 2,000 all-white students. The school is air-conditioned, carpeted, and has the latest in curriculum materials and multi-media instructional aides. A discussion is occurring in a classroom studying a new American history unit on Black Studies. Each student has on his desk a copy of *Leadership in American Society: A Case Study of Black Leadership,* one of the Episodes in Social Inquiry prepared by Sociological Resources for Secondary Schools and published by Allyn and Bacon, Inc. They also have a copy of *Negro Views of America,* a unit prepared by the Harvard Social Studies Project and published by American Educational Publications. Both of these teaching materials are "inquiry oriented" and focus on skill development. The teacher, however, is not using the materials as they have been designed. She is carefully using the material to help the class come to an understanding and appreciation of the value of hard work, dedication, and upward social mobility. She has just had the class read in the A.E.P. unit a case study of Frederick Douglass, a 1930 interview with a former slave of an Alabama plantation, an excerpt from Richard Wrights' *Black Boy,* and a brief selection from the play *Raisin in the Sun.* The students have been vigorously discussing a Harlem gang leader's description of the life in an inner city ghetto. After reading of the poverty, despondency, and bitterness in Harlem, the teacher asked the students to hypothesize about why such deplorable conditions exist in America. And while a few students had been ineffectually trying to argue that the situation was a result of racism, they had neither the information nor the sophistication to adequately defend their ideas. The majority of students were suggesting that the reason for the ghetto situation in Harlem was that the people were lazy, ignorant, and lacked the necessary motivation to get either a good education or a good job.

The teacher interrupts the class discussion and concludes, "I think we have suggested a wide variety of explanations for the deplorable conditions of our inner city and have debated the pros and cons of each idea. I would like to summarize today's lesson by pointing out what I consider to be the salient concern in this whole issue and then give you an assignment for tomorrow. So if you will take out your pens and paper, you can jot down a few of my summary remarks." The class with a mild groan and a few furtive glances at the clock in the rear of the room, shuffled through their materials and in a few minutes was ready to take notes.

"I believe the most important thing to remember from our reading and discussions during the last few days is the fact that Black Americans who are willing to work hard and sacrifice can gain an education and rise to prominent positions of leadership in our communities and the nation. There are very few places in the world where this can happen. We are never free of prejudice, discrimination, and racism. But in America, hard work and dedication and sacrific can result in upward social mobility. Take for example Richard Wright, Claude Brown, Gordon Parks, Sammy Davis Jr., and so many more who rose above conditions they were born into and achieved greatness." She turned to the chalk board and began writing categories that included politicians, actors, writers, and athletes. "I would like for you to make a list of prominent Black leaders in each of these categories for class tomorrow. Try to think of several people in each list. I think you will be surprised how many you can list."

"As a background to tomorrow's discussion, I would also like for you to read through the Sociology Episode, *Leadership in American Society,* pages 12-52. These pages include brief case studies of Black leaders, both in the past and today. This reading should demonstrate that there have always been Blacks who have been able to succeed in America; even though they had to overcome poverty, prejudice, and slavery. As you read through these case studies, I would also like you to compare the strategies and philosophies of two groups of Blacks. One group includes Martin Luther King, Roy Wilkins, Whitney Young, James Farmer, and organizations such as NAACP, SCLC, The Urban League, and CORE. The other is composed of men like Nat Turner, Stokely Carmichael, Malcolm X, and organizations like SNCC, the Black Panthers, and the Black Muslims. I think you will see that those groups that have worked within the system have demonstrated far more success than those who chose more extremist, revolutionary techniques. As you read, try to hypothesize about why this seems to be true, and think of information that supports your arguments."

During a recent visit to a local social studies classroom, another teacher was found to be using new materials to transmit traditional laissez faire values. A simulation game was just being completed by a group of 10th grade geography students. The students had been using the Metfab simulation.[17] The simulation provides students with voluminous data about a number of cities in the United States and also provides detailed role-playing situations for students. The goal of the game is to decide in what city the Metfab factory should be located. For several class periods the students had been studying natural resources, tax rates, transportation systems, and had engaged in intense decision-making discussions. While the simulation is designed to provide an opportunity for students to discover the intricate complex relationships between geography, transportation, and manufacturing, the teacher was using the instructional materials to teach the student the "greatness" and "fantastic freedoms and opportunities" of the American free enterprise system. Even the most sophisticated instructional package can be used by a teacher to help transmit desired beliefs and values.

Methods of Citizenship Transmission

More important than the citizenship transmission *content* is the way in which that content is *used and interpreted* by the teacher. The critical factor in citizenship transmission is the method of instruction and there are at least three distinctively different instructional approaches to this particular learning goal.

1. *Direct Transmission:* The simplest approach to citizenship transmission is exposition. The teacher used the read, recite, and remember approach to textbook study, supplemented by interpretive and inspirational lectures. Since the "authorized" content of our heritage is clearly defined in textbooks and course syllabi, the teacher will often drill students on the essential information over and over again until they have learned it. A point of of view that was popular in the 1920's went as follows: Decide what is important. Emphasize it. Drill it. And then drill it again. Satisfy yourself that your students will carry it with them to their graves.

While research suggests that few people will carry the bulk of knowledge transmitted in social studies classes to their graves, this fact has failed to dampen the effort or enthusiasm of many teachers. But even as students are reading and memorizing and trying to remember the "essential" information, the teacher is interpreting the information and instructing students in the proper attitudes and values they should have about the information. The teacher not only is the ultimate authority, he is the social agent responsible for cultural transmission. He demands that his students learn without question the "proper" interpretation and the "accepted" feeling they should have about the interpretation. Thus, direct citizenship transmission

56

occurs in the following manner:

a). The teacher selects the content, usually from authorized "sources," that demonstrates the desired lesson.

b). The teacher omits content that might well call into question the desired lesson.

c). The teacher transmits the content, usually via textbook readings, textbook assignments, class discussion of textbook assignments, and lectures.

d). The teacher interprets the content in lectures that are persuasive and often inspirational.

e). The teacher also instructs the students in how they should feel about the interpretation.

f). The students are then tested to determine how well they remember the content, accept the interpretation, and feel toward the content.

Teachers may even break down basic values into behavioral objectives so that they can observe whether or not students have truly internalized the designated value. For example, a teacher attempting to teach the "dignity and worth of the individual" might define the behavioral expectations in the following manner:

a). waits until others have finished speaking before speaking himself (does not interrupt others);

b). encourages everyone involved in a discussion to offer his opinions (does not monopolize the conversation with his arguments);

c). revises his own opinion when the opinion of others are more solidly grounded in, and supported by, factual evidence than his own (does not blindly insist on his own point of view);

d). makes statements in support of others no matter what their social status (does not put others in embarrassing, humiliating, or subservient positions).

2. *Indirect Transmission:* Many teachers who perceive their role as that of citizenship transmitter, approach their task in a much more indirect and subtle manner. They may carefully select and organize and omit information so that students might "discover" the correct interpretation and the proper values.

Such teachers may honestly consider themselves inquiry teachers who are teaching students effective thinking skills.

Teachers may also use the techniques of behavior modification to reinforce "acceptable" behavior, beliefs, and to condition students to desired learning outcomes. Such efforts might include praising and rewarding students who approximate desired values and behavior and labeling students who do not learn acceptable behavior and values as "discipline problems." An inquisitive and independent student who raises questions and asks for verification of a teacher's interpretation might be considered a disruptive student and disciplined accordingly. Students who raise their hand, demonstrate proper respect for the authority of the teacher, and behave as expected may be praised and rewarded. A bulletin board in an elementary school visited recently contained a name in the middle of a star announcing that the student was the "Good Listener of the Week," an obvious effort to condition students to be quiet and attentive to the teacher.

3. *Inquiry-Oriented Transmission:* Other teachers may be actually working to teach students the inquiry skills of effective thinking and research, except that they prescribe a number of overriding "givens" that are not to be questioned. These "givens" take on the quality of universal, unquestionable truth and define the areas in which inquiry can and cannot proceed. These "givens" may also be used as a "court of last resort," to alleviate intellect and value conflicts.

Students may inquire into corrupt election tactics, problems of juvenile delinquency, drug abuse, antiquated institutional practices, etc., but the student is not allowed to inquire into whether or not democracy is the best political response for dealing with these same issues. The student must accept as givens that all of the hypotheses that might be suggested for dealing with a particular problem must be consistent with democratic procedures. The value of democracy itself remains unquestioned. In a similar vein, these universal values may be used to alleviate value conflicts. During the recent Viet Nam War a group of students were discussing a news story entitled "U.S. Troops Won't Go Into Battle." The story explained that

U.S. troops in Viet Nam had refused to obey an order to go into enemy held areas to collect materials and equipment that had been left during a rapid transfer of men. The soldiers explained that the order put the risk to human life far beyond the potential gains in equipment. After identifying and discussing the issue in value terms, the students concluded that the conflict was between "obedience to higher authority" and "self preservation." The discussion concluded by appealing to a higher value, the worth and dignity of a human life. After it was concluded the equipment could be replaced without jeopardizing the lives of soldiers and civilians, the class felt the soldiers were justified in their actions. Thus, a "universal" value was used to alleviate the conflict.

Some feel that there are some values that cannot be proved and must, therefore, simply be accepted. Donald Oliver and James Shaver, who have done much to encourage the teaching of inquiry skills and value analysis and to encourage the use of public controversy as the content of the social studies, have indicated they believe that the central commitment in our society is to "promote the dignity and worth of each individual who lives in the society."[18] They explain this basic value in the following way:

> We find it basically impossible to justify or rationalize in any ultimate sense *why* individual freedom and human dignity *should* be the central objective of the society. Not only does such rationalization on a philosophical level inevitably become regressive and circular, but anthropological evidence suggests the extent to which the persuasiveness of 'reasons' depends on the culture in which one is reared. There is no final proof on such a value; when one pushes to the heart of human values, he must invariably end up accepting some tenet on faith. Recognizing the impossibility of breaking loose entirely from the structures of one's culture, even if one desired to do so, we see in the commitment to human dignity an explicable affirmation of the belief in man as an end in himself. We frankly accept the value of human dignity as a societal goal in a society in which that commitment

is central.[19]

Such an overriding value commitment thus became a determining factor in *all inquiries and value conflicts*. For Professor Shaver the "fixed moral principle" has to do with the necessity of regarding every person with dignity and according each individual equal rights. For instance, in a round-table discussion with other social studies educators, Shaver stated that

> I would be very upset if a child in my class said, "people do not have a right to equal opportunity. It is a ridiculous notion." I would have the feeling that this child is out of touch with reality, that perhaps his home and his education had failed him.[20]

Were a child indeed to utter these words, we would expect Professor Shaver -- consistent with his belief that any solution to a human predicament must reflect a fixed moral principle -- to draw the line at this point and to persuade the student that he is out of touch with reality and ought therefore to adopt a more realistic point of view. Precisely what is the difference between this approach and indoctrination in a given value is not clear. Probably there is no difference.

Pushing this issue even further, Joseph Junell argues that value conflicts cannot possibly be resolved and alleviated solely by the intellectual processes of reflective thinking.

> I do not argue with the general excellence of ... (reflective thinking) ... What I do object to is the implication that truly meaningful solutions to problems which involve conflicting values can be reached without reference to some pre-established framework of commonly held moral absolutes ... The need to teach reflective techniques is not in question here. Critical thinking should inform every proposed solution to the human predicament. But the solution itself must be the direct reflection of some fixed moral principle pinpointed somewhere on a scale of primary values.[21]

Critical Evaluation

Although the Citizenship Transmission tradition reaches back into antiquity, the instructional goals and techniques associated with this approach are still dominant today. Citizenship Transmission is the single most important mode of social studies found in our nation's classrooms and is enthusiastically endorsed and supported by many professional organizations and by community groups. Indeed, the more core social values are challenged by different organizations and articulate spokesmen, the more warmly many endorse some form of rigorous instruction in basic moral values.

The single most grave problem associated with this position, as we have already stated in this chapter, is the difficulty in reconciling it with the tenets of democratic social philosophy. No matter how benign the intent of a Transmitter or how firmly a given value is regarded as altogether proper, good and right, Citizenship Transmission, no matter how qualified, *begins* with the assumption that there are right answers, right beliefs, good values, and worthy traditions and that it is the student's responsibility to integrate these into his total outlook. There are, of course, other difficulties with this mode of social studies teaching.

Transmission collides head on with the realities of a pluralistic society. While there are, to be sure, basic values that most would agree represent our democratic tradition, the pluralistic nature of our society tends to be ignored. The existence of social stratification, of different races, economic theories, social philosophies, regional traditions, and sectional interests are usually overlooked. Transmission teachers ordinarily assume that what is either printed in the text or supported by some vague entity called "the community" is desirable and worthy of being transmitted. A given Transmission teacher might acknowledge the existence of, say, Black militants, woman's rights advocates, non-Christian beliefs, socialism, etc., but these tend to be regarded as deviations from the core values that must be transmitted. In short, Citizenship Transmitters ignore the reality of value conflict in our society, a reality that leaps at anyone who reads newspapers or watches TV newscasters.

Something else is also ignored. By and large, the average Citizenship Transmission textbook is out of touch with most forms of scholarship in the social sciences. Using one example, it took American history text writers more than 30 years to acknowledge that there was more involved in America's entry to World War I than German submarine warfare. By the same token, while civics textbooks are still mired in a neutral and objective description of the structure and function of governmental institutions, most political scientists have abandoned this approach decades ago.

The end effect of much Citizenship Transmission is distortion -- intended or unintended. Complexities are glossed over, issues are not acknowledged, problems are omitted --very often as a deliberate policy on the part of publisher or State or local curriculum committee. After 12 years of schooling, students tend to grow into an uncritical admiration for American history, ideals, celebrities, and institutions. So important is it to convey or support a particular point of view that the undeniable difficulties of our existence are denied.

Finally, the largely unconscious desire of Transmitters to persuade, describe, and to mold their students into an ideal of a good citizen means in practice that student needs and interests tend to be given short shrift. Teachers, by and large, hold that it is important to enlist student interests and to deal with their needs. But, they ordinarily complain, it is difficult to do this and to also "cover" the prescribed material. In fact, the material is not prescribed, as is usually believed, for State curriculum laws and State adopted syllabi are neither widely read nor understood and do not usually detail concepts to be covered. Thus, the teacher who states that he would love to deal with something "interesting" but obviously cannot because of the necessity to reach page 576 by the end of May has --utterly without his conscious awareness -- been persuaded that the most important thing in the world is the necessity to transmit a set of ideals, facts, and beliefs. This teacher is not usually aware of the origin of these beliefs, but he knows that some overwhelmingly important imperative demands that he transmit what he himself learned.

Thus, despite most social studies teachers' nod toward the goals of critical thinking, problem-solving, decision-making and the like, the dominant mode of teaching is the uncritical transmission of selected ideals and beliefs. The origin of the transmission process is the necessity of the culture to survive. Whether the omission and distortion inherent in Citizenship Transmission indeed guarantees cultural survival is another matter.

NOTES

[1]Joseph Junell, "Intelligence Without Morality,"*Phi Delta Kappan,* XLIX (September, 1967), p. 43.

[2]Jack Anderson, "Rediscovery, Rededication,"*Atlantic Constition* (August 17, 1973), p. 45.

[3]*Ibid.*

[4]Robert D. Barr, "The Changing Role of History in the American Public Schools," (unpublished PhD dissertation, Purdue University, 1969), pp. 15-48.

[5]A wide variety of research conducted during the past 40 years had demonstrated the close relationship between school social studies programs and the transmission position.

[6]William T. Hartley and William S. Vincent, *American Civics* (New York: Harcourt, Brace and World, 1970), p. 201.

[7]Orrel T. Baldwin, *The Story of Our Nation* (New York: Noble and Noble Publishers, 1970), p. 201.

[8]Lawrence Kohlberg, "The Moral Atmosphere of the School," *The Unstudied Curriculum: Its Impact on Children,* ed. Norman V. Overly (Washington, D.C.: Association for Supervision and Curriculum Development, NEA, 1970), pp. 104-127.

[9]"Transmission of U.S. Heritage in Peril." *Bloomington* (Indiana)*Herald Telephone,* (October 25, 1969), p. 26.

[10]*Promising Practices in Civic Education* (Washington, D.C.: National Council for the Social Studies, 1967), p. 10.

[11]Committee on Concepts and Values, *A Guide to Content in the Social Studies* (Washington, D.C.: National Council for the Social Studies, 1957), p. 73.

[12]William H. Cartwright, "What is Happening in the Social Studies," *Social Education XVII* (February, 1954), pp. 77-79; and James High, *Teaching Secondary School Social Studies* (New York: John Wiley and Sons, Inc., 1962), p. 209.

[13]See specific content recommendations found in Edgar B. Wesley, *American History in Schools and Colleges*, Report of the Committee on American History in Schools and Colleges of the American Historical Association, The Mississippi Valley Historical Association and the National Council for the Social Studies (New York: Macmillan Company, 1944).

[14]Elizabeth G. Kimball, *A Survey of the Teaching of History and Social Studies in Secondary Education* (Princton, New Jersey: Educational Testing Service, 1969), pp. 2 and 5.

[15]Harold J. Noah, Carl E. Prince, and C. Russell Riggs,"History in High School Textbooks," *The School Review,* LXX (1962), p. 436.

[16]Jonathon Kozol, *Death at an Early Age* (New York: A Bantam Book, 1967), p. 67.

[17]Association of American Geographers, *Geography in an Urban Age*, Six Units, (New York: Macmillan Company). For a complete listing of the contents, see *El-Hi Textbooks in Print*, (New York: R. R. Bowker, 1975), p. 58.

[18]Donald W. Oliver and James D. Shaver, *Teaching Public Issues in the High School* (Boston: Houghton Mifflin Company, 1966), p. 9.

[19]*Ibid.*

[20]*Concepts and Structure in the New Social Science Curricula*, ed. Irving Morrisett (New York: Holt, Rinehart and Winston, Inc.), p. 72.

[21]Junell, *op. cit.*, pp. 43-44.

CHAPTER III

Social Studies Taught as Social Science

As the teacher finishes repeating instructions, the twenty two second graders split into two groups, eleven of them hurrying to a large round table and eleven of them to three rectangular tables placed end-to-end. The teacher walks to the back of the room and joins a man with whom she has been planning this day for several weeks. The children have been coached to anticipate a "fun time."

All of the boys and girls chatter loudly, comparing their opinions of the assortment of gauze, bandages, mercurochrome, cotton swabs, tape, and tongue depressors with each other. Each child at the round table examines the piles of items and begins to select one from each pile, carefully placing it in a large white box with a red cross on it. The children standing at the tables placed end-to-end are performing a slightly different task: they are lined up evenly, each opposite a pile of identical items. They have been told that each of them is to put one item in the box and then give it to the next child who is to place another item in it and in turn pass it on. Obediently, the first child puts cotton swabs in the box and passes it on to the next one who places the gauze in it, and so on.

The children play the game, obviously intent on what they are doing, for fifteen minutes. Teacher then announces that this part of the game is over and directs their attention to the two piles of filled first aid boxes. Will one child please count the number of filled boxes by the round table? And who wants to count the number of filled boxes by the end-to-end tables? And will another child please go to the chalkboard and write down how many both groups have packaged?

The boys and girls mill in circles, wander, talk animatedly to each other and nevertheless succeed in reaching their seats. The teacher catches their attention as the man in the back of the room watches every detail carefully, making mental notes of each step of the unfolding process. As soon as they finish the prerequisite question--Did you all enjoy doing that?--the teacher begins to ask, first about the activity and then about the figures on the board, figures which clearly indicate that the boys and girls at the tables placed end-to-end have packaged something like three times the number of first aid kits assembled by the children at the round table. The chorus of protests dies down, for it becomes apparent that the difference between the two figures is not a function of one group's goofing off. The teacher is not quite ready to reveal what does make the difference, but she will do so in a few days. There is no reason, she has been convinced, that her second graders cannot both use and understand the economic concepts "division of labor" and "specialization."

History of the Tradition: Immediate Background

For "division of labor" and "specialization,"terms usually associated with a basic course in college economics, are precisely what the children are learning. There is nothing novel about teachers who use games to teach concepts, for educators are familiar with the term "activity curriculum" and have used enjoyable routines for many years. What is novel is the sophisticated concepts these seven year olds are being asked to learn. Why has "Our Friend the Mailman" given way to two complex economic concepts? Of what value is it for very little children to learn that individual workers assigned to perform one small task in an entire production sequence can turn out vastly more units than can workers who build an item from the ground up?

Similar questions were asked a few years ago by Lawrence Senesh, an economics professor from Hungary, whom journalist Martin Mayer has described as an American educational genius. In the view of Senesh--and many others who were soon to share a common set of assumptions--the social studies curriculum commonly taught to children from ages six to eighteen was indefensibly stupid, fragmented, and empty. The bits and pieces of history and government, the aimless busy-work ranging from building pyramids out of clay to visiting city hall, had little to do with an understanding of, to use his own words, "the dynamic changes of our society." It had less to do with intellectual development. And, as millions would attest, it

66

was stupendously, endlessly dull

Senesh, at the time a professor of economics at Purdue University, soon gathered associates and students.The climate was right; many educators and laymen were ready for change, and the government was in a proper mood to distribute millions of dollars to anyone who would describe how a lifeless subject could be infused with new purpose. Equally important, Senesh could rely on the writings of Harvard psychologist Jerome Bruner, whose *The Process of Education* was to pave the way for a host of curriculum reformers.

Senesh, as we have said, was not alone, Scholars from history, geography, political science, sociology, and anthropology had reached almost identical conclusions. All agreed that the collection of cliches and rhetoric called social studies was not worth teaching. All felt that the solution to the question, What should be taught and how? was to be found in an examination of the disciplines of each of the social sciences.

Convinced that existing social studies was ineffective, provided with a workable rationale for organizing and teaching a new social studies curriculum, social scientists needed only to attract support, assistance, and money. This was to happen almost immediately.[1] For at this moment in our history, the government began spending millions of dollars. Distributed by the United States Office of Education and the National Science Foundation, money was found to sponsor clinics and workshops, fund organizations and finance pilot curricula. As organizational activity proliferated, the original curriculum reformers were joined by scholars who were similarly imbued with zeal. Graduate students came to study under these scholars, and soon journals, books, monographs, papers, and multi-media packages were rolling off the printing presses. Teachers were informed, cajoled, and persuaded, and many of them agreed to give the newer materials a sympathetic try. By the end of the decade of the 1960's it was possible to talk about a truly "New" social studies.

History of the Tradition: 19th Century

But the promising "New" social studies being developed in the 1960's was far from new. In fact, it represented a tradition of social studies education that dated back to the late 1800's when historians and social scientists began not only to take a searching look at public school curricula, but to convene "blue ribbon" commissions and committees to make recommendations about what *should be* taught in the public schools. And it came as no surprise that what they wanted taught was solid courses in history and what was even then recognizably social sciences.

Such interest in revising the public school social studies was not only to attract the major professional organizations of historians and social scientists, but some famed scholars in these academic disciplines. Such eminent historians as Henry Johnson, Carl Becker, Charles Beard, and James Harvey Robinson set out to see that history was to be taught in the schools, and taught well. Moreover they even developed what was to be called a "New History" that they hoped was to be more useful and relevant to students and society. As early as 1915, Henry Jonson was demanding that social studies classes stop transmitting myths and propaganda and teach instead academic history. What did Johnson propose to teach? The answer is: historiography--how an historian goes about historical inquiry. He also emphasized the process of historical development. Both of these goals would emerge, some fifty years later, under the auspices of the "New" social studies.

During the late 1800's, American historians became actively and professionally interested in school social studies programs. During this period, historians took a commanding position in outlining the content of school social studies programs. Since the social sciences were only beginning to develop as independent academic disciplines, the historians were in control. What they recommended was predictable. Students should study history for the sake of studying history as an end in itself. And, they should study copious amounts of history. Such recommendations emerged quickly and commandingly from a series of committees and commissions held under the auspices of the American Historical Association. There was the Madison Conference of the NEA Committee of Ten (1892), and the AHA Committee of Seven (1899), Eight (1907), and Five (1905). What was recommended was a series of four blocks of history at the secondary level:

9th grade - Ancient History

10th grade - Medieval and Modern European History

11th grade - English History

12th grade - American History

The "block approach" to history exerted a tremendous impact not only on the public school curriculum, but on textbooks, course syllabi, and college entrance requirements. The Committee recommendations provided the first semblance of order in the social studies curriculum in the United States. The goal of teaching history was identified as citizenship but a concept of citizenship that was to differ markedly from that employed in most public schools. Students were to become better citizens by virtue of the content and methodology of history, the prevailing assumption being that learning "basic" subject matter was essential for competence in civic affairs. This emphasis on subject content was a reflection both on the historians who made the recommendations and on the need for preparing public school students for college. The Committee's recommendations yielded a significant effect in secondary schools and was to set the basic patterns for public schools to follow until a decade and a half into the 20th Century.

But the historians were not alone. Such distinguished scholars as the political scientist Charles E. Merriam and Harry Elmer Barnes, the sociologist, were also attracted to the nascent reform in the social studies.

And while there was conflict and infighting between the American Historical Association, the American Political Science Association, and the other social science organizations about the specific content of social studies courses, there was almost unanimous agreement that public school students should learn the structure and inquiry processes of the scholarly disciplines.

After a brief period which found professional educators exerting the dominant influence in public school curriculum development (see Chapter IV), the historians and social scientists returned. In an attempt to ensure that public school social studies continued to rest on the academic disciplines, the American Historical Association called upon social scientists to join with educators to build a unified social studies program.

69

The result of this call was the formation of the Commission on the Social Studies in Schools which was initially assembled in 1929. The Committee boasted some of the most eminent social scientists and educators who were to conduct one of the most comprehensive and thorough analyses of the social studies ever to be undertaken. The Commission Report filled seventeen volumes and established a new direction for school social studies. But while the Commission encouraged schools to focus social studies courses on student interest and societal issues, the foundation continued to be solid social science. Students were to be encouraged to practice the social scientists' method of inquiry through the study of primary sources, analysis of historical interpretations, forming of basic concepts, and composing of their own history. Students were to learn the methods of inquiry, scrutiny, criticism, authentication, and verification.

By the early 1960's the other social science disciplines had matured into strong academic disciplines that began challenging the historians' traditional influence on the public school curriculum. When the Federal and Foundation money began to arrive, the newer social scientists wheeled into action to develop what they felt would be a truly new and different social studies, one based on the nature and processes of their academic disciplines.

The Social Studies Taught as Social Science: Purpose

Although virtually all of the social scientists[2] have spoken to the question, To what end ought social studies be taught? their answers are somewhat unclear, perhaps because they are usually couched in the term "understanding." The National Task Force on Economic Education in 1961, for instance, stated, "Economic understanding is essential if we are to meet our responsibilities as citizens and participants in a basically private enterprise economy." Other writers tend to speak in the same way. Thus two social scientists associated with the Educational Services Incorporated say, "The aim of the E.S.I. junior high school course is to understand the development in America of a distinctive political culture..."[3]

One historian says, "Raising fundamental questions about the nature of history in the interest of interpreting human

70

society is indeed a legitimate goal of historians."[4]

One sociologist named Gresham Sykes says, "The study of the professional sociologist, is primarily a matter of transmitting a systematic knowledge of a scientific discipline."[5]

The purpose of high school social studies, says Sykes, has been taken to mean the promotion of citizenship. And this, as we have already seen, is an ambiguous position. Sykes argues that professional sociologists wish students to possess an "integrated" view of society, no matter how elementary this view may be. For only in this way can students gain an idea of society through a coherent body of thought.

These statements, although none of them are entirely clear, do share something in common. There is a pattern to the use of such terms as "understanding," "interpreting," and "an integrated view of social processes." What these terms might mean could perhaps be summarized in the following sentence: The social scientist wants young people to perceive the world through the eyes of a social scientist, to ask the kinds of questions that a social scientist asks, and to use the analytical tools and concepts of the social scientists.

The social scientist believes that if a student acquires the habits of mind and the thinking patterns associated with a particular social science discipline, he will become more discriminating, make better personal as well as social policy decisions, and, ultimately "understand the structure and the processes of our society."[6]

The question the reader should now ask is, What do you mean "think the way social scientists think?" To answer this question, we will have to examine, rather too briefly, the way social scientists go about gaining new knowledge.

When a social scientist looks at the world, he does not do so through the eyes of a layman. Laymen tend to rely on their own personal experiences and observations and infrequently on a systematized body of knowledge. Laymen are loaded with unconscious prejudices and biases. Laymen jump to conclusions and reach unwarranted generalizations. Laymen confuse cause for effect, facts for theories, observations for inference. Laymen are, in short, unsophisticated and undiscriminating. The social scientist, by comparison, has a large and tested body of con-

71

cepts, analytical tools, procedures, and investigatory processes. It is these which he wishes to teach young people. Let us move from these admittedly abstract statements to some particulars.

When a cultural anthropologist looks at the world, he tries conscientiously to go beyond the limits of his own culture. He knows that most persons in a given society tend to think that what they see around them is "normal," "natural," and entirely proper. That which deviates from what they see is "perverted," "immoral," or perhaps merely "crazy." A cultural anthropologist has been examining many different cultures for many years and is able to compare and contrast behavior within these cultures. Thus, when he talks about social control, he does not just mean the British common law that most of us are accustomed to. He also refers to the social control mechanisms of Eskimos, of Kwakiutls, of the Arapesh, and the Pilaga. He is not just talking about social control of industrialized, Westernized, Christian, democratic, and capitalist societies. He means to refer to a wide variety of different societies. By the same token, he does not believe that the American nuclear family is the only kind of family setting that exists. Peoples in different parts of the world have lived successfully with all sorts of family arrangements including various forms of polygamy. Our sexual codes are not the only ones in the world. All peoples have some kind of regulations governing sexual behavior but these regulations vary widely from culture to culture. It is this variance--and the need to look at variance in a neutral, objective, nonjudgmental fashion--that cultural anthropologists wish students to acquire. For cultural anthropologists look at the world in this way, they find it satisfying and productive; they believe it gives them a much wider and more precise perspective on human behavior. And to repeat our point, it is this way of looking at variable behavior that the cultural anthropologist wants young people to acquire. From the standpoint of cultural anthropologists, the sooner and the more thoroughly they acquire it, the better off they will be.

The Social Studies Taught as Social Science: Method

The following is an illustration of how such an anthropologist might conduct a lesson. A group of social studies students in a

10th grade world history class were crowding into a black, 1964 Ford. There were too many students for the small car, and the crowding was made more severe by a tangle of tape recorders, notebooks, file folders, and even camping gear. They began yelling and waving at their teacher in a car just in front of them, where several other students were still trying to get a similar jumble crammed into the trunk. Finally, everything was packed, and all were ready to depart. The teacher hurried back to the car in the rear and after a final warning to drive carefully and the usual instructions about what to do in case they became separated, the small caravan drove off.

The students were bound for an over-night camp-out at a religious commune called Padanoram, located in Bedford, Indiana. The students had contacted Daniel, the patriarch of the commune, and arranged for the class to visit Padanoram to talk with the people in the community. The class had been studying the observation technique used by anthropologists and felt itself ready to attempt their own comparative cultural study. These students had already spent the night in an Amish home and following the Padanoram camp-out and inquiry, they had plans to replicate their investigation with a group of people who operated a local "health food" restaurant and bakery and who called themselves an Ashram community. The students were attempting to identify the beliefs of these groups and then to make a comparative analysis in which these beliefs would be compared with their own. The students were fascinated by the different child-rearing practices, the different roles of women, and even the life goals of the various groups.

By the time they had completed their observations, gathered their data, and written the final report, the students not only had acquired an impressive amount of information and had developed insight into three cultural groups, more importantly, they had learned an organized method of perceiving social phenomena, and gathering, recording and analyzing raw data.

Let us now turn to other social scientists and examine their unique ways of perceiving the world. For an economist, life is perceived as making economic decisions. "In fact, in large measure, economics *is* our life," as Professor Lewis maintains.[7] For economists the primary, inescapable assumption about life is scarcity. Individuals, economists assert, express unlimited desires, but resources are always inadequate to satisfy such desires. In the words of one economist, "The fact of scarce resources poses the over-all *economic problem* (italics in original) that faces all societies and dominates all economic situations and issues. It also poses the task of the science or discipline of economics."[8]

As we might now anticipate, economists assert that given the limited means at hand, we "are forced to be concerned about how our means are used, what goods they are used to produce and in what quantities, and in what proportions the goods are to be distributed among us all..."[9] Man, therefore, is forced to choose.   The task is to devise some satisfactory way of economizing, of making the best choices possible. Given these unavoidable economic realities, we must make decisions about inflation, taxation, foreign aid, growth rate, public health, full employment, and thousands of other issues.

Not to be aware of the inescapable fact of scarcity is to foolishly believe that we can have whatever we want and that there is no cost involved. To be unaware of scarcity and choice-- of the need to economize--is to assume that simple preference and desire are enough. When economists look at ecologists harassing manufacturers because factories foul our air, they tend to respond by advising: instead of staging ineffectual demonstrations, environmentalists ought to look at the root causes. Our society desires many goods and products which only a highly industrialized manufacturing economy can produce. Our industrial system is based upon the capitalist assumption that any entrepreneur deserves to make a profit. To dump waste products into streams, to allow smoke and chemicals to escape into the air has seemed to make economic sense. It has been considered economically cheaper to dump waste into a stream than it is to treat it through some complicated and expensive process. The industrialist is only maximizing his profit. If one really wishes to analyze the *social costs* as well as the ecological costs of air pollution, he should discover who pays these costs and what it will take to clean up the environment. Economic analysis of this sort will yield a much more accurate picture of reality than merely shrieking at manufacturers. If young people can learn to look at the world this way, they will gain a much better, more useful understanding. It is the teacher's job to teach students how to analyze real problems in the real world. Consider another illustration.

Caught in the midst of spiraling inflation and an increasing scarcity of basic commodities, a 12th grade economics class considered a field-study of the local economic situation to determine the effects of federally mandated controls on retail prices. Organizing the class into a group like "Nader's Raiders," the teacher and her students began a careful analysis of the relationship between price controls and commodity scarcity. The students identified a number of commodities they wished to study--poultry, beef, and gasoline. They also developed a detailed plan of investigation. They identified five supermarkets in their area and ten local service stations, representing six major oil companies. They began a series of interviews with the managers of the stores and stations and gained price information both before and after the price freeze. Later they visited wholesalers and warehouses, and even interviewed farmers and cattlemen in the area. They supplemented their interviews with statistical information about the declining availablity of products. They also studied economic trends published in national magazines and newspapers such as *U.S. News and World Report, Fortune* and *The Wall Street Journal.* The students were able to develop specific hypotheses about the relationship between the price freeze and commodity scarcity, and to gather sufficient data to reach intelligent conclusions.

The present day historian naturally entertains his unique view of the world. This, says Haskins,[10] involves scientific method but must also be considered an art. The historian's job is to reconstruct the past in as imaginative and accurate a way as possible. Historians set for themselves problems which involve gathering data, evaluating primary and secondary sources and reaching valid interpretations. The way historians proceed is a model for all of us when we begin thinking about historical events.

Specifically, when an historian examines a particular historical event, he does not leap to a conclusion after viewing the first piece of evidence. He gathers a wide variety of evidence, including letters, diaries, official orders, court depositions, personal reminiscences, and newspaper accounts. He does not simply accept any given piece of historical evidence as demonstrated, proven fact. He wants to know, Who wrote this diary and what sort of man was he? Was he an honest person and an objective observer? Or did he have an ax to grind? What was the climate of opinion at that time? And did it influence the gathering of information? Is this document really based upon second hand information? Is the document, in fact, a forgery? Historians also believe that every age writes its history consistent with its own particular views and beliefs. Historians perceive, for instance, that one generation of Americans saw the American revolution as essentially a struggle over political liberty while another age viewed it in the context of a desire by colonists for more economic autonomy. Any historian must, therefore, be aware of the particular intellectual climate in which all historians work. It is the refined and systematized awareness of large historical frameworks and of the specific means by which historians gather data and make inferences that is the historian's particular contribution to the education of Americans. It is not merely the particular facts and interpretations recorded in a textbook that is significant. It is the intellectual operations used by historians which all school children ought to acquire. And to repeat the point once more, the sooner young people acquire these, the better off they will be. Let us turn to another classroom example to illustrate this point.

The 11th grade U.S. History class was arranged in several small groups clustered in a seemingly disorganized manner around the classroom. The students were involved in a wide variety of apparently unrelated activities, accompanied by the usual classroom rumble. The class, in fact, resembled the kind of functional chaos one might find in the city-room of a newspaper or a political headquarters on election night. Some students were arguing animatedly over a conflicting issue. Others were quietly reading through a stack of copies of old news stories. Three students were at the chalk board and appeared to be developing a chronological sequence of events from a clutter of scribbled notes. In the rear of the room a small group of students huddled around a tape recorder, occasionally switching off the machine to discuss what they had been hearing and to take notes.

The teacher is sitting on his desk reading several pages of typed narration. He pauses occasionally to ask questions of two students standing by him, and to jot down comments and grammatical corrections on the margin of the paper.

The teacher, in his fourth year of public school teaching and concurrently pursuing an M.A. degree in the field of U.S. History during summers and evenings, has brought his love of history and historiography into his social studies classroom. Several days previously, he brought to class a number of primary historical documents and spent the entire class period describing an historical event that he thought might interest his students. He explained that while researching the 1929 Depression in their local community, he had discovered an extremely interesting and even mysterious event that seemed to have been overlooked by historians and long ago forgotten. At that point he asked the students to put away their pens and pencils, to sit back and relax and let him share with them a fascinating story. He plunged into a provocative account about a local Communist organizer named T. E. Barlow, who had been arrested in Fort Worth, Texas in the early 1930's. He described the man, gave a number of humorous annecdotal accounts of this "Texas Communist" who was by profession a farmer and who wore overalls to organization meetings. He told of Barlow sending telegrams to "Ma Ferguson," Texas' only woman governor, and finally of being arrested and held in the Fort Worth city jail. The teacher was a first-rate story teller, and soon his students were engrossed in the reconstruction of the past. They occasionally laughed at the teacher' humorous stories about Barlow and even began to interrupt with questions. Finally, the teacher reached the climax of his story. "It seems," he said, "that sometime during his first night in the Fort Worth city jail our 'Texas Communist' was killed." He quickly followed this by recounting the known information about the event and passed around copies of several news stories reporting the event. He likewise read a number of "letters to the editor"

77

and two editorials that appeared at the time. Quickly he began involving the students in the intrigue and excitement of the case by raising a number of conflicting hypotheses about the case. Had Barlow been murdered by the local police or had he died in a fight with a fellow prisoner? Had Barlow tried to get arrested in order to gain publicity for his cause; and did he try, once jailed, to create a situation in which he could accuse police of brutality? The teacher also began to identify a number of mysterious, unanswered questions which seemed to enthrall the students. Soon a lively discussion was underway.

Out of this beginning, the teacher carefully encouraged the students to "write the history of T. E. Barlow." He shared all the material he had gathered, and then began listing on the chalkboard information that they felt was essential to resolving their questions. They also began to develop a list of sources of information. The next class period found the students beginning to organize for their own historical inquiry. One group of students was to visit each of the three local newspapers and read through a thirty-day period to search for relevant news stories. Another group planned a visit to the local police department to gather information. Other students began listing the names of all the people involved in the Barlow event; they also listed the names of people who had written "letters to the editor." They prepared a list of city officials--the mayor, city council members, police chief, etc., and assigned the task of discovering the names of these officials at the time of Barlow's death. Within a few days, the classroom was alive with activity. Principals in the case had been identified and had been contacted by mail. Police files and newspaper storied had been duplicated. At this point, students entered the initial stage: framing a number of theories. Some students had decided to reconstruct the social setting of the time and were listing the movies that were being shown at local theaters, describing cultural events that were occuring during the period, summarizing major news stories of the time, and even studying contemporary fashions.

Throughout this investigation, the teacher constantly pushed the students to find missing information, locate essential witnesses, speculate on why some individuals refused to talk to them about T. E. Barlow, and to judge the validity of their evidence.

After three weeks of intensive investigation, the class concluded their inquiry and had written a history entitled, "Whatever Happened to T. E. Barlow? A Study of the Death of a Texas Communist." The study was carefully documented and footnoted and included transcripts of interviews, copies of official documents, and even pictures. The students even began laughingly to refer to themselves as "junior historians."

These descriptions of a variety of the social sciences, accompanied by illustrations of how teachers might realize social science learning goals in their classrooms, should serve to indicate the kinds of intellectual and instructional operations associated with this particular social studies position.

All social science teachers and curriculum makers have an idea of the desired set of intellectual operations that they want to teach. We do not have space to summarize all of them, but suffice it to say that sociologists, geographers, psychologists, and political scientists also have clear notions as to the thinking patterns they wish students to acquire. In the next section, we will discuss *content* and illustrate what is meant by this term, with actual examples from currently used social studies curricula that have been designed by social scientists.

The Social Studies Taught as Social Science: Content

Our concern in this section is to answer the question, What kind of content do social scientists consider proper for the curriculum? We have made the traditional distinction between "content" and "method," but only for purposes of convenience. In reality, content and method are not separable. However, as we use the term content here, we mean something like the actual subject matter -- the ideas, concepts, theories, principles, assumptions that social scientists consider important.

In reality, most public school social studies teachers who perceive themselves operating in the social scientist tradition, utilize as their most consistent and dependable content, the college lecture, notes, texts and readings from their university history and social science courses. For many social studies teachers this reliance on the academic discipline for course content is a natural process. Viewing the dated and distorted public school textbooks with disdain and contempt, these teachers have discovered their own university notes and records more dependable and often more interesting. The social science teachers tend to teach those ideas and processes that were taught to them. What the university professor feels is important later becomes the content agenda for the public school teacher. Since many social studies teachers understandably entertain a good deal of respect for their former university professors, they attempt to emulate them in their own classroom. Many join the American Historical Association, American Political Science Association, the American Sociological Association or other professional social science organizations. They do no think of themselves as social studies teachers; in their eyes, they are historians and social scientists who happen to be teaching in secondary schools rather than universities or colleges. Since the social science teacher finds his university materials accurate and detailed, he may often use this store of knowledge to "debunk" the myths that the textbooks often portray. The textbooks' never-told-a-lie-George-Washington becomes a red-headed, foul-mouthed, slave-owning, sexual adventurer who even wore an ill-fitting set of wooden false teeth. Harding's administration is highlighted with stories of his wife, "the Iron Duchess" and talks of illegitimate children, poker games, and hints of death caused by arsenic poisoning. The textbook grandeur of the Spanish American War gives way to the military fiasco of an imperialist administration. And on and on. Such intellectual "debunking" is usually received quite well by the surprised and amused students and thereby sends the teacher scurrying for more "inside" information on heroes and heroics of our nation's past.

Other social science teachers will use their college lecture notes almost verbatim as ready made course outlines and teaching plans. They emphasize concepts and generalizations, and may even involve their students in sholarly research studies and surveys, writing local history, and gathering statistical data.

The reader will get a clearer idea of social science content if he contrasts it with an example of traditional content. Recall from the first chapter that most content of those whom we call "Citizenship Transmitters" tends to consist of separate chapters, traditionally conceived, and organized in the same fashion

80

that writers have organized them for years. For instance: virtually any textbook on U. S. History begins with a chapter called "Our European Antecedents." It usually goes then to a chapter on European exploration and then to one on colonization. There is usally a chapter on the growing conflict between the colonists and the English king and Parliament. The chapter on the American Revolution is followed by one on the problems of the new nation, and then by one on the westward movement, or perhaps Jacksonian democracy. This organization proceeds inexorably until it reaches contemporary American history, omitted in the textbooks of the 50's and 60's but included in the 70's with reference to such problems as McCarthyism, racial relations, conflict over foreign policy, changing sexual mores, etc.[11]

In fact, U. S. history textbooks generally have been organized this way for years. The only difference between a text written last year and one written ten or even 30 years ago, is that the older ones do not get to World War II or the New Deal. Most civics textbooks follow some version of the original civics text, the Magruder work, which has gone through close to 60 editions. Most texts on economics, sociology, and other courses are organized in the same predictable fashion, with the same chapter headings and approximately the same information. The only differences are the wording, the choice of visuals and the color of the binding.

The social scientists who contemplated curriculum revision within the last ten or fifteen years wanted both a different set of concepts and a different mode of presenting them. Let us look at some fairly typical examples of current social science secondary curriculum materials.

First, let us examine the book of readings called "Patterns in Human History" from a series prepared by the Anthropology Curriculum Study Project, a division of the American Anthropological Association.[12] This particular set of readings has the theme Modernization and Traditional Societies. The reason for this is that cultural change is a typical anthropological problem and many cultural anthropologists are interested in what happens when a "traditional" society attempts to become "modernized" and industrialized.[13] What we see first is that this paperback is magenta. Inside the paperback are collections of readings and pictures that carry a good deal of emotional impact. The drawings are equally expert. The chapters in this book of readings do not even remotely resemble the usual explanatory, didactic text. There is no attempt to describe a variety of concepts objectively; rather the readings consist of standard ethnographic material. Ethnography is a division of cultural anthropology. Roughly it consists of the anthropologists' description of the day-to-day life of a particular culture, written by a field worker who has actually lived there, who has learned the language and has tried to understand behavior from the inside. Ethnography is the name for the way anthropologists go about gathering data on cultures. The first chapter, "Life in Hasanabad, Iran," is a very well written and interesting account of a small town in Iran. The reader learns of the daily life of the people here--the planting and gathering of crops, the various rituals and rites, the system of land-ownership, education, and the stratified class system. A chapter a few pages later, "Marriage in Ireland" attempts to make sense out of the concept of bride price by interviewing the bride's and groom's parents and then explaining how dowries actually function in rural Ireland.

The book of readings, designed for students, is accompanied by a separate guide for teachers. Each of the various units contains a teacher's guide which includes rationales, suggestions for lesson plans, activities, and discussion questions. The magenta colored teacher's guide contains an overview, which, among other things, tells the teacher that "this basic orientation provides some ideas and tools for observing and recognizing patterns in human behavior." This is entirely consistent with the anthropologist's basic assumption that what students ought to know are the conceptual framework and categories--the "ideas and tools"--by which anthropologists classify human social behavior.

The teacher looks at the first chapter called "Peasants" and finds in the lesson plan the statement that, "Students' understanding of 'the state' and its assumption of all force and authority is essential to any understanding of peasants and the process of modernization." (p. 6, Lesson One, Teacher

Background, Teaching Plan, Modernization and Traditional Societies.)

Other than the attractive packaging, two important characteristics of this example of social science curriculum should be noted. First the materials do not consist of information *about* peasant culture. Instead, there are actual anthropological data, very similar to primary source material compiled by anthropologists. The data consist of on-the-site ethnographic description of actual people in a real place. Second, the teacher's guide asks students to employ a particular anthropological construct: students should be able to identify the cultural forces which define the life of peasants. These two characteristics perhaps exemplify the main difference between social science curricula and conventional material: the social scientists make every effort to employ the raw data of their investigations; social scientists want students to ask the same questions, using the same categories that they themselves employ.

A brief look at the "Episodes in Social Inquiry Series," a unit from a series entitled Sociological Resources for the Social Studies, would also be helpful in illustrating social science curricula. This curriculum project was sponsored by the American Sociological Association. Note, now, that the anthropological project described above was sponsored by the American Anthropological Association. The pattern ought now to be emerging: professional associations of social scientists have had a major hand in sponsoring, defining, and creating the new materials.

The Social Inquiry Series[14] materials consist of a variety of multi-media material: The episode entitled *Migration Within the United States* contains an instructor's guide, a student manual, a printed handout consisting of tables and graphs concerning migration and a small vinyl record entitled "Students Discuss Migration." The teacher's guide contains directions to the teacher and the student manual consists of a preface, essays, graphs and charts, case studies, newspaper accounts, questions and conclusions.

In the Instructor's Guide, Section Two, "Who Are the Immigrants?" the authors describe the information in the student manual, interpret it, and make a series of suggestions for teachers. For instance: "The urbanization of Black Americans has been a dramatic phenomenon. Most people do not know that about 10 percent of all Blacks have moved from rural to urban residences in each of the last four decades, compared to only 4 percent of the whites. The class should have a stimulating discussion focusing on this difference in rate."

Other titles from the Social Inquiry series include:
Leadership in American Society: A Case Study of Black Leadership
The Incidence and Effects of Poverty in the United States
Testing for Truth: A Study of Hypothesis Evaluation
Social Mobility in the United States
Social Change: The Case of Rural China
Science and Society
Small Group Processes
Religion in the United States
Family Form and Social Setting

There are other titles, but these will illustrate the point. *All of these titles reflect the problems which professional sociologists examine.* Poverty, scientific method, social mobility, social change, the relationship between science and the social setting, small groups, religion, and family structure partly define the concerns of professional sociologists. It is these concerns which, translated into readable, interesting, lively curriculum material are the content of social studies defined as social science.

Let us now look at Geography in an Urban Age,[15] a curriculum project prepared by the High School Geography Project of the Association of American Geographers. This, too, is a multi-media project and is organized much the same way as the sociological and anthropological material you have seen above--case studies, problems, raw data, maps, and activities.

For a moment, we will again contrast this with a conventional geography textbook. A traditional text tends to be developed by area: a given area, say, Europe, S.E. Asia, Africa, North

America, etc., is described according to latitude, longitude, exports and imports, industrial capacity, racial composition, agricultural potential, climate, topography, etc. The end effect is extraordinarily dull and repetitious. The low-level generalizations and fragmented facts have little lasting value for students.

Geography in an Urban Age is different and the difference is obvious as soon as one examines the table of contents. It consists of the following:

Different Ideas About Cattle

Games Illustrating the Spread of Ideas

A Lesson from Sports

Expansion of Islam

Canada: A Regional Problem

Culture Change: A Trend Toward Uniformity

Why these topics? "Different Ideas About Cattle" demonstrates that different cultures make very different uses of the same resource. The cartoon illustrated an ancient peasant using an ox for plowing, a Spanish bullfighter, a steer marked for butchering, a pair of oxen drawing a cart, and a cowboy riding a Brahman bareback in a rodeo. Since geographers are concerned with the diffusion of cultural traits across land masses, the chapter entitled "Games Illustrating the Spread of Ideas" is a natural. Since geographers are also concerned with the interactions of cultures, the example of Canada as an illustration of the contact between French and English civilization is also entirely understandable. These topics--to make the point again--reflect the living concerns of practicing geographers.

These illustrations could be expanded to include the dozens of new social studies projects that have appeared, were field tested, and are now being commercially distributed. To summarize: The new social science material was conceived by professional social scientists with the assistance of the government and professional associations. The packaging reflects multi-media influence and consists of a wide variety of attractive case studies, pictures, problems, and raw data. The actual content of the materials reflects quite accurately the problems and concerns of practicing social scientists. The material is not merely descriptive but tends to include a good deal of the primary source materials of social scientists. The teacher is encouraged to ask students to solve the kinds of problems that are posed by social scientists, using the categories and processes invented by social scientists.

Method: Transmitting the Social Scientist's View of the World

In this section we will concentrate on what we have already referred to as the "habits of mind" that social scientists wish students to acquire. The new material is so constructed that the content--the problems selected by social scientists--is inextricably linked with the method--the means by which these problems are taught. Each of the social sciences can claim its own unique problem-solving procedures. And it is these procedures which are to be taught by teachers; for problem-solving techniques flow logically from the problems presented to students. There is one important exception, however, which we must note now.

For many years social studies teachers, who received much of their training from university professors of social science, employed an expository approach. That is, for the most part, a civics teacher dusted off his notes from his university classes in political science. These notes were meshed with the high school syllabus and the teacher then simply described to students the mass of information--the principles, facts, concepts, and theories--which he had learned. There was not the recent concern for hypothesizing, selection of data, inference, logical analysis, and so forth. Without really thinking about the intellectual procedures of the social science disciplines, the secondary teacher hoped that his description of the content would have some lasting effect. It is unlikely that it did and the general ineffectiveness was one of the major factors in the rise of the newer social science approach to the social studies.

Let us now examine some recent social science materials to see more clearly what method has been employed. Edwin Fenton, a professor from Carnegie-Mellon Institute, has been one of the most active proponents of the social science position. Receiving a doctorate in history from Harvard University, Professor Fenton--as we have already described the pattern--

turned his attention to the teaching of history at the secondary level. He has written college methods textbooks, lectured widely, trained graduate students, supervised a number of history projects and is one of the most widely recognized exponents of the "new" social studies. Along with Richard Brown's Amherst series, the Carnegie-Mellon curriculum materials perhaps most closely reflect the social scientist's conception of social studies.

A widely used Fenton text, *Teaching the New Social Studies in Secondary Schools, An Inductive Approach,*[16] deals extensively with the methods used by historians to gain knowledge. In the introduction to a chapter entitled "Teaching the Mode of Inquiry: History," Fenton asks, "How can we teach students to think like historians? Clearly we must devote a substantial proportion of our class time to this pursuit. We cannot leave the teaching of historical method to incidental learning while we concentrate in class upon amassing factual information."[17]

In a succinct paragraph, Fenton describes what he takes to be method:

> ...we must teach methods of interpretation if we claim to teach history. Students must learn the rules by which historians collect evidence and use it to interpret the past if they are to read or write history intelligently. They must be able to judge whether an author's conclusions are supported by the evidence he presents. They must also learn to draw their own conclusions and to present the evidence on which these conclusions are based. Unless students are taught to interpret, they are not taught history at all. Teaching the mode of inquiry of history and the social sciences lies at the heart of the new social studies.[18]

The following section spells out this important theoretical position in detail. History is not merely a narrative account of past events. It "...is primarily a way of thinking, a set of rules and procedures for making interpretations."[19]

Using some of his own essays and those by other historians, Fenton illustrates and explains such concepts, as, How does the historian classify information? How does the historian prove an hypothesis? How does the historian decide what is fact? How does the historian ask questions? How does the historian deal with a mind set?

A high school world history textbook[20] developed under the supervision of Fenton is arranged in very much the same fashion. There is almost none of the conventional didactic material, interminable descriptions of political, military, and diplomatic events with end-of-chapter questions usually stressing fact-recall information. Rather the book is filled with readings, interpretive essays, and questions designed to enable students to acquire some of the specific skills mentioned in the previous paragraph. Primary source material (that is, historical documents such as diaries, letters, traveler's accounts) that has been simplified for students dominates the entire text. The student does not read about, for example, the medieval period: he examines a document written by a contemporary person who describes the nature of the tribute paid by a peasant to the lord of the manor. He does not merely read a description of the rise of absolutism in France; he reads an account written by Louis XVI's minister of finance.

Interspersed with these first-hand accounts are questions designed to stimulate student thinking. The questions revolve around the authenticity of the documents, the kinds of assumptions held by the writers of the documents, the possible hypotheses raised, the nature of proof offered and the tenability of conclusions.

Almost identical to Fenton's concerns is a Social Inquiry series entitled *Testing for Truth: A Study of Hypothesis Evaluation.*[21] The table of contents reveals the sociologist's intellectual operations. The chapter headings are:

> Forming Hypotheses and Making Predictions
> Writing Questions and Questionnaires
> Sampling
> Administering Questionnaires
> Tabulating Results
> Analyzing Data
> Forming Conclusions and Generalizations:
> Reviewing the Methods Employed

Just as Fenton is concerned with students gaining insight into the limitations of primary historical sources, this Episode emphasizes the sociologist's tools. Sociologists rely heavily on questionnaires, are concerned with random and stratified sampling techniques, analyze data statistically, and check their procedures and conclusions.

The chapter on questions and questionnaires is, in fact, a handbook which a conscientious student could use to design his own data-gathering instruments. It begins with a problem: the hypothesis that boys will be more supportive than girls of a campaign for greater student participation in policy-making. It presents the reader with two alternative ways of asking a question and then asks him which one is better and why. It cautions that the questions should be clear to the respondent, and then defines the term "respondent" in sociological terms. It then deals with structured interviews and describes pitfalls to avoid. It covers the problem of differences in proportion of sexes and provides ways of dealing with this statistically. Ways of recording answers are then described and illustrated. The chapter concludes by calling attention to a later chapter on the use of Chi Square techniques and other elementary statistical methods.

In the Anthropology Curriculum Study Project, which we have already examined, the student is familiarized with primitive tools such as choppers, scrapers, cutters, and projectile points. He is then presented with a site map, a map divided into precise squares in which location of artifacts, the direction in which they point, the names of the artifacts and the dimensions of the site are laid out, precisely as they would be by an anthropologist or archaeologist who wishes to find out more about a primitive tribe whose remains he is excavating. The student is then asked to perform certain tasks, after which the teacher asks him to make inferences based upon the artifacts he has "discovered" and "plotted" on the map. What, for instance, could one tell about the food gathering techniques of this tribe? Did they hunt or were they agriculturists? What can one infer about the level of organization? Was it fairly complex, resembling those which hunting cultures tend to develop?

Similarly, *MACOS,* Man A Course of Study, another anthropological project, asks students to simulate living for many weeks among the Netsilik Eskimos. Students see brilliantly colored pictures of Eskimo life, go with Itimagnark on a seal hunt, explore the cooperative relations that seal hunts require, enact a play dealing with attitudes toward old age and mating, construct tools and weapons out of clothespins, an, in other ways, explore in very considerable depth the meaning of one Eskimo culture.

The MACOS curriculum has recently (in 1975 and 1976) been much in the news. Both the popular press and the professional journals have reported a good deal of controversy directed against numerous aspects of MACOS, especially its treatment of death, abandonment of the elderly, and sexual mores of the Netsilik.[22] The criticism has been voiced that the treatment--which its proponents would describe as conventional anthropological cultural relativism--would appear to give sanction to values considered unacceptable by the majority in this culture. Proponents have responded by claiming that such constitutes gross misunderstanding of MACOS. The authors are not concerned with settling the argument, but we would make two observations. First, there is, we would argue, consistent with our position so far in this text, a good deal of miscommunication between the professionals in the field and the public: the professionals see MACOS as simply dealing with a conventional anthropological "problem;" opponents see such treatment as undermining conventional beliefs, i.e., mores and values traditional in this society. Second, the bulk of the criticism has come from those whom we have labeled Citizenship Transmitters. Some of the Transmitters--both in and out of the teaching profession--have made their position extremely clear: by *not* condemning abandonment of old people, polygamy, etc., the MACOS curriculum writers have, in effect, seemingly approved such practices. The argument, we suggest, has not been drawn well, partially, of course, because of the extraordinary level of emotion and excitement that has been aroused, and partially because of the underlying fear of Citizenship Transmitters: study, any kind of inquiry, exploration or investigation of held values, will lead to erosion of *those values*.

To summarize: The method advocated by the social scientist

is based upon one central assumption: that students should learn the specific ways that a particular social science discipline has evolved to gain new knowledge. Whether it is the discipline of history, political science, anthropology or whatever, the student is to learn about hypothesizing by formulating hypotheses. He is to learn about data-gathering by examining the kinds of data that the social scientists gather. He is to learn about the testing procedures by asking the kinds of questions of the data that social scientists actually ask. He is to learn about conclusions and proof by examining the logical processes used by economists, geographers, and all other disciplinarians. This is exactly what Professor Fenton meant by the quotation which you read on page 87: "Teaching the mode of inquiry of history and the social sciences lies at the heart of the new social studies."

Critical Evaluation

Recall that the social science tradition is actually two historically distinct traditions--before the 1960's when teachers essentially transmitted what they had learned from their social science professors, and after 1960, when we can clearly identify a well defined position based upon the assumption that students would best be prepared for citizenship if they but learned the ways of knowing developed by social scientists. As the translation of the findings of social science researchers, this tradition is no better or worse than any other transmission process. Piling on of uncalled for information ordinarily results in a high degree of boredom, listlessness, and forgetting. However, the more than 120 New Social Studies projects which are based upon some kind of Brunerian notion deserve a more detailed criticism.

First and most obvious, it is difficult to evaluate all of the many New Social Studies projects turned out by different organizations in a fifteen year span. The existing statistical data we have seen used to evaluate these projects are not especially conclusive. It is difficult to "prove" that a given program results in significant learning or indeed accomplishes what its creators intended.

We would rather rest this critical evaluation upon an analysis of the major assumptions of those who believe that social studies should be taught as social science: that the most appropriate and fitting content derives from the social science disciplinarian's problem. As we have already stated, the social scientists who directed the development of new social studies materials shared the same basic assumptions. Professor Lawrence Senesh, a leading exponent of the Social Science tradition tells us, "The primary function of the development of analytical thinking is to help our youth understand the structure and the processes of our society.... In the final analysis, the purpose of social science education is the development of problem-solving ability." However, just what is signified by the phrase "development of problem-solving ability" is by no means clear.

In another work, two of the present authors suggested that the problem-solving done by adult citizens centers around social problems and public policy problems. That is, citizens are called upon to make decisions about desirable public policy relating to crime and delinquency, poverty and defense. At this moment, for instance, the public is being called upon to establish policy concerning whether the government ought to take a more aggressive role in economic matters or whether our present economic recession will clear up of its own accord, responding to the operations of the free market system.

We now wish to point out that the class of problems selected by those we designate advocates of the social science position have selected problems that are only distantly related either to social problems or to public policy problems. Sociologists and criminologists studying crime are more likely to select a problem such as, "What is the nature of reported crimes committed by Jewish males (second generation Japanese, middle-class Blacks, or women between the ages of 21 and 35)?" Another typical social science problem might be, "Do women receive lighter, the same, or harsher sentences for identical crimes committed by males? The Social Scientist curriculum materials are organized around problems which, like this one, reflect their own usually persisting interests and concerns.

However, while it is easily granted that the data unearthed by social scientists are of considerable practical use to legislators, to judges and to administrators in the making of public policy, it is by no means clear that students who study a social scientist's problems are thereby better equipped to make decisions, i.e., to solve problems. The social scientist's selected problem is abstracted from the confused welter of social phenomena. It is demonstrably of interest to social scientists to amass wide-ranging data on many different elements of a problem.

However, there is no reason, on the face of it, to believe that students who conceptualize a social science problem and imitate the social scientist's data-gathering procedures and analyses are thereby better able to decide what *ought* to be done in the realm of public policy.

The assumption--to the best of our knowledge hitherto unchallenged -- that by studying the disciplinarian's problem, students will be more effective in making decisions in the realm of public policy is, at best, undemonstrated. This assumption constitutes an article of faith. Social scientists are concerned with shedding more light on different types of behavior--not necessarily for the purpose of ameliorating any social problem (although, of course, their data may lend itself to precisely this use) but simply for the sake of the research itself. And many social science researchers continue to accept what is known as "value-free" methodology. That is, they attempt to avoid value judgments and to gather data and perform analyses in as objective and dispassionate a maner as possible.

Without raising the knotty philosophical issue of whether a "value-free" assumption is tenable, we should simply like to conclude with two observations. First, the students' concern for social problems, far from being rooted in value-free analysis, springs primarily from bias, prejudice, conviction, and belief. Second, most of the curricular materials designed by social scientists either deliberately or unconsciously avoid value judgments. This is not the authors' casual observation: it is based upon a detailed examination of the contents and especially the questioning strategies actually used in social science materials. Our conclusion is that by a clear policy of issue avoidance, many of the social science materials probably miss the concerns of most students. That intellectually gifted students are likely to find many of the newer Social Science materials of interest seems to be a fact. That the majority of students are drawn to the concerns, problems, and techniques of social scientists, however, appears to be an assumption that is dubious, or at best, undemonstrated.

NOTES

[1]Not only did social studies curriculum reformers appear on the scene, but many others as well. The 1960's were full of new names, acronyms, and projects, e.g., BSCS, the Biological Sciences Curriculum Study, Chemstudy, "new" math. Curriculum reform took place in all subjects, grades, disciplines, and fields.

[2]We will use the shorthand term "Social scientists" for the more accurate but cumbersome "advocates of the position that the social studies ought to be taught as the social sciences."

[3]See Nona Plessner and Joseph Featherstone, "Political Science as a Structure for Social Science Curricula, *Concepts and Structure in the New Social Science Curricula,* ed. Irving Morrissett (New York: Holt, Rinehart and Winston, Inc., 1967) p. 105.

[4]See Ralph Haskins, "History," *The Social Sciences Foundations of the Social Studies,* eds. John U. Michaelis and A. Montgomery Johnston (Boston: Allyn and Bacon, 1967), p. 25.

[5]See Gresham M. Sykes, "Sociology," in American Council of Learned Societies and the National Council for the Social Studies, *The Social Studies and the Social Sciences* (New York: Harcourt, Brace and World, Inc.), p. 159.

[6]Lawrence Senesh, in *Concepts and Structure in the New Social Science Curricula,* ed. Irving Morrissett (New York: Holt, Rinehart and Winston, Inc.), p. 21.

[7]See Ben W. Lewis, *The Social Studies and the Social Sciences, op. cit.,* p. 109.

[8]*Ibid.*

[9]*Ibid.*

[10]Haskins, in Michaelis and Johnston, *op. cit.,* p. 34.

[11]Textbook writers in the past almost universally ignored the persisting and troublesome social problems within our society. This was not merely an oversight but a deliberate publishing policy. Within the last few years, it appears that a number of small publishers have become adventuresome enought to distribute problems-oriented texts, brochures and pamphlets which clearly examine such issues as changing sexual mores,

censorship, pornography and the like.

[12]Anthropology Curriculum Study Project, *Patterns in Human History Series,* (New York: Macmillan). See *El-Hi Textbooks in Print,* (New York: R. R. Bowker, 1975), p. 204, for a listing of the contents.

[13]Although, in fact, no one has explained the meaning of "traditional" and "modern" in a way that everyone accepts.

[14]American Sociological Association, *Episodes in Social Inquiry Series,* (Boston: Allyn and Bacon). For a complete listing of the materials and content, see *El-Hi Textbooks in Print* (New York: R. R. Bowker, 1975), p. 58.

[15]Association of American Geographers, *Geography in an Urban Age,* Six Units (New York: Macmillan). For more information on these units, see *El-Hi Textbooks in Print* (New York: R.R. Bowker, 1975), p. 58.

[16](New York: Holt, Rinehart and Winston, 1966). Fenton has since somewhat modified the position he took in this work.

[17]*Ibid.,* p. 151.

[18]*Ibid.,* p.151.

[19]*Ibid.,* p. 151.

[20]Edwin Fenton and T. Walter Wallbank, World History Program, *Thirty Two Problems in World History* (New York: Holt, Rinehart and Winston, 1969).

[21]American Sociological Association, *Episodes in Social Inquiry Series, op. cit.*

[22]See *Man: A Course of Study,* (Washington: Curriculum Development Associates, Inc., 1972). For an analysis of the conflict in two professional journals, see *The Kappan,* LVI (October, 1975) *79 passim,* and *Social Education* XXXIX (October, 1975), pp. 79-81.

CHAPTER IV

Social Studies Taught as Reflective Inquiry

The buzzing dies down as teacher begins the class session. "So. Did anyone happen to read yesterday's headlines?"

Arms rise in the air and a few hands wiggle energetically. "Who wants to tell us what they said?" the teacher inquires, addressing his question to no one in particular.

"The governor got busted. Ha, ha, ha," one youngster contributes. "The governor was arrested," the teacher repeats, changing the colorful idiom to more conventional English. "What is he charged with?"

Nancy reflects for a few moments, and languidly raises her hand. "He really isn't arrested. He is being sued by someone for bugging his telephone."

"All right," the teacher comments. "Anything else?"

"Yeah," Earl adds helpfully, "some guys from the State bugged this guy's phone and he's suing the whole state."

"One moment," cautions the teacher. "Is it a fact that these State officials bugged someone's phone? Or are they merely charged with doing so?"

"Well, they caught these guys with the electronic stuff, what do you want anyhow?" Harold says, obviously annoyed at the hairsplitting.

"Well, we will probably have reason later on to talk about an idea we looked at recently called 'assumption of innocence,' but for now, we can summarize by saying that some State officials from the governor's office are now being sued for planting an illegal telephone tap. Would all of you agree that this is, as far as we know now, a fair statement?"

Some students nod their heads affirmatively. Others sit, unclear as to what the teacher is driving at, but willing to go along for a little while longer. A number of teenagers are staring out the window, not visibly concerned with governors, legal suits, or illegal bugs.

"Now," the teacher continues, "we need some more information. Who is suing those officials?"

"Some radical, I don't know. Some guy."

"Does anyone know a little more about this man," the teacher persists.

John leans over to confer briefly with another student. In a moment, both raise their hands. The teacher recognizes John.

"I don't know his name, but he's some kind of black militant or other, and he said that the governor's office or someone had been bugging his phone and that he's going to sue them," John strings together the information breathlessly.

"Well," the teacher responds to John, "that's about the way I understand it, too. Now, why is this man suing these officials?"

Harold, who has already expressed impatience with fine distinctions about assumptions of innocence, speaks again. "For bugging his phone. We already know that."

"We know about the telephone tap. But, why is there a law suit? Was a law broken?"

There is more silence. A few of the window-gazers decide to join the rest of the class. Most of the class are clearly confused, as is obvious from the furrowed brows. The teacher says nothing, merely waiting for someone to respond. Eventually someone does.

"You aren't supposed to bug anyone's phone."

"Why not?" the teacher probes.

"Because the law says you aren't."

Again the teacher waits for this to sink in. No one else speaks, so he questions again.

"However, it has already been established that the governor's appointed officials, men from the attorney general's office, are involved. Do you mean to tell me that these men broke the law?"

The question is clearly provocative and instantly three or four voices break in at once.

"No, no, if the attorney general taps a phone, it isn't breaking no law."

"Look, this guy was a radical!"

"So!" exclaims a student, although it is unclear whether he intends to refute the statement that the complainant is a radical or that the State attorney general's office is incapable of violating the law. There is a crescendo of buzzing and stage whispers. The teacher waits for a moment for the hum to die down.

"Now, just a minute. What's the confusion?"

Nancy again slowly raises her hand and attempts to pinpoint the issue. "An illegal telephone tap," she says with finality, "is not legal. No matter who does it. Not even the police."

This piece of legal philosophy is immediately challenged. "Nancy," one student asks, more an accusation than a query, "are you in favor of letting a bunch of radicals bomb things without trying to do anything about it?"

The teacher smiles inwardly. The issue is joined. He begins to think of the next phase of his questioning strategy.

The teacher knows just what he is about. The first few minutes of questioning were designed only to pave the way for the "hooker," a problem that both grabs the class's attention and generates a sense of confusion. The teacher is aware that many Americans feel that whatever the "government" does to protect itself from subversion and sabotage is legitimate and defensible. He also knows that many Americans express revulsion at the idea that "Big Brother," whoever this is, may be listening in on their private conversations. That both ideas are in mutual conflict the teacher understands quite well; that many individuals do not perceive the conflict he also understands. The objective of his questioning strategy is to bring this conflict out in the open, to encourage students to express their personal beliefs, and, as soon as possible, to encourage what he takes to be a process of inquiry.

It is fairly evident fact, however, that virtually every teacher, at every grade level, and in every subject matter field also feels that *he is* encouraging the process of inquiry. The situation is not unlike that of the great comedian, Jimmy Durante, who, periodically, would stop his patter, look to heaven imploringly and rasp out, "*Every*body wants to get inda act." Everybody does want to get in the act. Every teacher would like to feel that, in some sense, he is encouraging students to think, to reflect, to engage in inquiry. However, it is clear that not everybody agrees on the proper definition of the terms "think", "reflect," or "inquire."

Those whom we have described as advocates of the Citizenship Transmission position advance their own claims to inquiry. As they see the process, it is essentially one in which the teacher, whose maturity and fund of information are far more developed and extensive than students, performs the primary thinking processes. It is the teacher who acts and interprets the information. Students are encouraged to pattern their own thinking and acting after the teacher's model. For those whom we have described as Social Science advocates, it is the teacher who presents the information and indicates the process. The student's job is to act, that is, to take the information and use it according to the social science model that he is being asked to accept and incorporate into his own thinking processes. Those whom we call advocates of Reflective Inquiry believe that the students should both interpret and act. That is, they should use the information--interpret it according to certain criteria--and decide what actions, or consequences and implications are to be selected. However, these distinctions are not especially obvious and when a social studies educator gets up in front of teachers and encourages them to take a crack at inquiry, most teachers respond, at least inwardly, "Absolutely. You are so right. Inquiry is the thing. And, furthermore, I do it!"

Inquiry-- From the Standpoint of Those Who Advocate Reflective Inquiry

Even though inquiry is not a term whose meaning is agreed upon and shared by all, we still choose to use the term. Definitions of "inquiry," "reflection," and "thinking" have multiplied over the years like hangers in a clothes closet, but we will select the following: "Inquiry as a method means that a teacher and his students will identify a problem that is of con-siderable concern to them--and to our society--and that relevant facts and values will be examined in the light of criteria."[1]

This definition is important not only for what it includes but also for what it is specifically designed to exclude. We are not talking about "covering" a topic without deviation, as for instance, reading all chapters of a textbook in order. We are not talking about the social scientist's approach to inquiry, which involves essentially the learning of a mode of research based upon the procedures of a particular scholarly discipline. The emphasis in this definition is, first, on dealing with the clearly sensed, felt, and perceived problems of students; second, on relating these problems to a wider social context; and third, on applying relevant data according to specifically stated criteria, criteria which are derived from what is known as the "scientific method of thinking."

History of the Tradition

Unlike the social science position which was sired by distinguished academicians in history and the social sciences, Reflective Inquiry has always been the bastard child of the social studies. Even the Citizenship Transmission position, while being more plebian in heritage than that of Social Science, arises out of significant and identifiable nationalistic sources. It has been watched over and guarded by no less than the Daughters of the American Revolution, The Council for Basic Education, the P.T.A., the N.E.A., patriotic politicians, and even by the man on the street, the mythical John Q. Public. In comparison, Reflective Inquiry has been like an abandoned child crying in the wilderness. It has enjoyed only a sporadic, isolated sort of support and, more unfortunately, it has tended to bring out the worst in its opponents. Whenever there has been an educational witch-hunt, you may assume that Reflective Inquiry was sure to be fingered, inevitably dragged out and burned along with John Dewey, Progressive Education, and other morally lax bed-partners. Even as late as 1957, when the launching of Sputnik I set off panic among Americans, the public had to "dig-up" a villain. As Postman and Weingartner so aptly put it, "John Dewey was just beginning to get comfortable in his grave when the Russians reached down and stuck a spear in his heart."[2] Dewey's crime, of course, was all that "gooey, romantic, permissiveness" that had somehow been mistaken for Reflective Inquiry. Inevitably caught in the crossfire between patriotic indoctrinators and rigorous academicians, Reflective Inquiry has been little more than a scapegoat in the history of social studies during this century.

Professional organizations have avoided it, few teachers have ever used it or even seen it in operation, and it continues, for some social science educators, to be the most difficult to define and most complex of the three traditions. During the last 75

100

years, when the position was emerging, there have been only a few scattered dissertations and a half-dozen books that have ever developed the concept, and some of these were concerned primarily with the philosophical and psychological foundations of the idea. Specific teaching recommendations and illustrations have been limited to only one professional committee in 1916 and a handful of social studies educators writing since the mid-1950's. But wherever it has been described or discussed, it has inevitably been done in relation to the nature of contemporary society, for it was out of efforts to develop a social studies program responsive to the problems and issues of the modern era that Reflective Inquiry came into being.

As first the Industrial Revolution and then the Electronic Revolution swept through our culture, ripping it loose from its small-town, rural beginnings, we were assaulted with increasingly rapid shock waves of dramatic social change. Once again, Postman and Weingartner, referring to this phenomenon as the "Change Revolution," describe it well:

> In order to illustrate what this means, we will use the media again and the metaphor of a clock face. Imagine a clock face with 60 minutes on it. Let the clock stand for the time men have had access to writing systems. Our clock would thus represent something like 3,000 years, and each minute on our clock 50 years. On this scale, there were no significant media changes until about nine minutes ago. At that time, the printing press came into use in Western culture, About three minutes ago the telegraph, photograph, and locomotive arrived. Two minutes ago: the telephone, rotary press, motion pictures, automobile, airplane, and radio. One minute ago, the talking picture. Television has appeared in the last ten seconds, the computer in the last five, and communications satellites in the last second. The laser beam--perhaps the most potent medium of communication of all--appeared only a fraction of a second ago.[3]

Such dramatic and continuing social change has exerted a powerful effect on all of us. It has created value conflicts, inter-

and intra-personal disputes and contributed to psychological confusion. Alvin Toffler diagnosed this condition by coining the phrase we have become so familar with--"future shock."[4]

Social change is not the only important characteristic of our contemporary society. Settled originally by people of diverse origins and outlooks, our nation has always been a pluralistic mosaic of competing groups. Nothing so typifies our culture, according to some authorities, as conflict--conflict between capital and labor, young and old, social classes, racial groups, and, of late, between the sexes. Such conflict has been intensified by the continued industrialization of our country and the accelerating rate of social change.

Accompanying the conflict and social change of the contemporary period is yet another important development. This is referred to as the "knowledge explosion." Some estimate that man's knowledge is doubling every two to three years. New disciplines have been developed within existing disciplines. Besides the development of the new social sciences, the field of history is also proliferating. Such fields as archaeology, epigraphy, carbon dating, and astronomy are uncovering more and more of the distant past, and with the passage of each day and week, history is inexorably extending. New knowledge, information, and insights lead to reinterpretation of former "truths." Much, therefore, that has been formerly accepted as valid information is later rendered obsolete. Even historians are somewhat bewildered by the vast transformation in the field of history. Allen Nevins says that "powerful new forces are at work in the field of history" and "few men understand the half of them."[5]

Taken together, these three characteristics--rapid social change, group conflict, and the knowledge explosion--created an educational crisis in curriculum development, especially in the social studies area where teaching had largely been limited to what we have called Citizenship Transmission and Social Science.

Since the earliest time, educators viewed the purpose of the school as transmitting accumulated wisdom (values and academic knowledge) to each new generation. Such practices seemed logical since it was assumed that each new generation would live substantially the same as the previous generation. But Alfred North Whitehead maintained in the early 1930's that "We are living in the first period of history for which that assumption is false."[6]   More recent, but less sophisticated thinkers have agreed. Margaret Mead has argued that social change is so great that man has become an "immigrant in time," and that children find it increasingly difficult not only to learn from parents, but even from older brothers and sisters.[7] Marshall McLuhan likewise maintains that because of social change the present is "more like the electronic future than the mechanical past," so he argues it is more useful to study the future than the past.[8] The Reflective Inquiry position maintains that such a situation has rendered the Citizenship Transmission position extremely tenuous. The analogy of the clock serves to illustrate this point.

> There are some teachers who think they are in the 'transmission of our cultural heritage' business, which is not an unreasonaable business if you are concerned with the whole clock and not just its first 57 minutes. The trouble is that most teachers find the last three minutes too distressing to deal with, which is exactly why they are in the wrong business. Their students find the last three minutes distressing--and confusing--too, especially the last 30 seconds, and they need *help*. While they have to live with TV, film, the LP record, communication satellites, and the laser beam, their teachers are still talking as if the only medium on the scene is Gutenberg's press. While they have to understand psychology and psychedelics, anthropology and anthropomorphism, birth control and biochemistry, their teachers are teaching 'subjects' that mostly don't exist anymore.[9]

Robert S. Lynd, the sociologist, said as early as 1939, "There never was an era when the appeal to history meant less."[10]   As long as our culture existed in rural, small-town settings with most students dropping out of school and only two percent going on to finish college, Citizenship Transmission and Social Science college preparation seemed reasonable and acceptable. But around the turn of the century, when the pace of social change

103

began picking up, a few philosophers and educators became increasingly concerned and that concern is even more intense today. The central question is, How can we transmit values in the midst of such agonizing social change? And given the conflicting pluralistic makeup of our country, which of the many heritages should we transmit? Especially today, when teachers are working with students who will only be middle-aged in the year 2,000, the question becomes, What can we teach students that will be of lasting value, that will not be quickly rendered inaccurate, obsolete and wrong? And how do we teach constantly expanding areas of knowledge? Or how do we decide what to teach and what not to teach? As educators have weighed these questions, increasingly the answers have pointed toward teaching students a process of Reflective Inquiry.

The first serious effort to develop a social studies program directly related to the conditions of contemporary society occurred in 1916. During this period, with scholars like William James, John Dewey, and E. L. Thorndike making major contributions, education slowly became a recognized field of study. Education was also becoming "professionalized" and educators were beginning to assert themselves in a more agressive manner. Strengthened by the philosophy of pragmatism and reinforced by research in education and psychology, a new concept of learning began to develop. The initiative that had belonged to the historians throughout the nineteenth century began to pass to educators who shifted their focus to the 90 percent of the students who did not go on to college rather than the 10 percent who did. The historians were startled to realize a significant shift had occurred. As one put it, "...leadership had plainly passed to militant educational reformers largely unhampered by scholarship in any of the social sciences..."[11]

Perhaps the most influential single person in the development of education during this period was John Dewey, the American philosopher and educator. Writing from an early background of a small rural New England town and from his experiences as an administrator of the nation's first laboratory school, Dewey was to develop the key aspects of Reflective Inquiry. Arguing that education should consist of transmitting neither the accumulated values of a culture nor the academic disciplines,

104

Dewey advocated that the school curriculum must grow out of the needs and interests of students. Schools should not attempt to transmit large bodies of irrelevant and largely useless knowledge; they should be helping children to live more effectively in their turbulent contemporary present. This could be done, Dewey argued, by helping students to develop more effective thinking and decision-making skills, by helping students decide what they needed to learn, and providing them with a systematic, scientific process of learning that they felt important. In a word, the Reflective Inquiry process grew out of a desire to help children learn how to learn and be more effective at this process. The significance of Dewey's ideas to the social studies was quickly apparent.

In 1916 the National Education Association convened the Committee on the Social Studies, and the very fact that the committee's name carried the term "social studies" was a clear indication that a dramatic shift had occurred in the area of social education. The Committee recommended that students were to become effective citizens not by memorizing historical content, but by practicing decision-making in their daily lives. The Committee saw subject matter not as an end in itself but as a means of reaching the goal of citizenship. But citizenship was not defined as obedience or conformity to certain norms, it was perceived as the development of "judgment," the ability to make rational decisions. Deciding that education was not simply to be preparation for adult life, the 1916 Committee recommended that educational experiences in the here and now were of maximum importance. The best way to train and prepare for citizenship for the future was to provide some opportunities to practice citizenship in the present. Thus, rather than studying only the past, current events and decision-making were emphasized.

In proposing these new goals of instruction, the Committee developed a revolutionary concept of the social studies.

1. Stressing that the social studies (including history) was to be "functionally concerned with the needs and interests of the present, the study of ancient and colonial history gave way to a stress of human welfare, vocational guidance, economics, and contemporary problems.[11]   To accomplish this goal, the Com-

mittee suggested two entirely new courses that were not simplified university disciplines. One they called Civics; the other Problems of Democracy. Both were to draw upon history and the social sciences for relevant knowledge. The Committee also recommended that two days per week be devoted to the study of current events.

2. Stating that history in the public schools should follow a social interpretation unhampered by chronology or geographical limitations, the usual method of arranging content according to historical chronology or separate courses in various disciplines was seriously questioned. The Committee recommended that the content of the social studies be organized around topics and problems. History and the social sciences were considered as a group of interrelated subjects combined under one course of study and could be used together in the investigation of contemporary problems. In order to achieve effective citizenship, problems should be studied, not history.

3. Even more revolutionary, the Committee recommended a new method of teaching. They recommended that the usual reliance on drill, exposition, and recitation be replaced by a method of problem solving. Rather than transmitting content, the teacher was to assist students in identifying and inquiring into problems.

4. The problems to be studied were to be selected from two sources: the immediate needs of the students and those problems of vital importance to society.[12]

These recommendations had the true ring of revolution, for they not only broke with the work of curriculum developers in the past, they were antithetical to all that had gone before. But like so many other revolutionary ideas, the initial effect was largely to generate a good deal of confusion and antagonism.

By the 1920's most public schools had accepted the 1916 course recommendations and were teaching Civics and Problems of Democracy. Current Events had also become an established part of the school program. But the revolution was largely deceptive, for many social studies teachers and social scientists continued to demand school programs modeled after university disciplines, and continued to debate with equal fervor the idea of decision-making, student needs and interests, and con-

106

temporary problem solving. But even more confusing, no one seemed to know how to teach a course focusing on decision-making. Even in those schools where new contemporary problems courses were developed, teachers continued to transmit conventional content as well as indoctrinate their values. The schools had adopted the curricular patterns of the 1916 committee but failed to employ their recommended method of teaching.

The problem was that few teachers seemed to identify exactly what Dewey or the 1916 Committee had in mind by the term "teaching decision-making." Some educators bought part of the Reflective Inquiry position and thought that Dewey, *et al.*, had simply been recommending new content. Rather than studying history and the social science disciplines, it was thought the social studies should focus on problems and therefore text writers and curriculum developers set out to identify the basic problems of our society and then have students study them. Thus "problems" became yet another area in which knowledge should be transmitted. A quick survey of most Problems of Democracy courses or "problems" textbooks invariably listed the same problems, and teachers set out to "cover" the problems as they had always "covered" the eras of history. Teachers lectured and drilled; the students memorized information about the problems. The problems studied were often as far removed from students' lives as a study of the Middle Ages.

Others tried a different approach. They looked at the lives of young people and tried to identify their personal problems. Some courses were even called "Personal Problems." These courses, once again, consisted of a series of substantive issues to be covered and ranged from pimples and petting to personal cleanliness. With enthusiastic teachers at the fore, students waded through yet another set of deadly boring and usually irrelevant information. Such efforts led to counseling programs and concern for the "life adjustment" of students.

While the concept of "problems" was disconcerting educators, others were experiencing similar difficulties with the "needs and interests" approach. Some educators, realizing they were older and wiser than school youth, set out to develop a curriculum based on "what kids need" to learn. This simple notion exercised an appeal to academicians who quickly argued that all students "needed" to know history and social sciences. Once again we were back where we started. Other educators, going straight to the source, asked young people what they needed to learn, only to be met by vacant, incredulous stares and shrugs of "I don't know." Still other teachers focused on utilizing student interest in the learning process, but found that students seemed only to be interested in cigarettes, athletics, cars, and one another. Undaunted, teachers tried vainly to extract out of these peripheral and transient concerns something intellectually worthwhile, and one soon found students studying "Sports in the Middle Ages," "Dating in the 17th Century," and "tracing the history of racing cars.."

By the late 1930's and early 1940's, the camps were divided and busily warring with one another. During this period, a president of the National Council for the Social Studies, Edgar B. Wesley, encouraged social studies educators to stop being "poor cousins" to the American Historical Association. For the first time, Wesley called on social studies educators to hold an independent national conference rather than continuing their practice of meeting as a yearly subgroup of the American Historical Association. Progressive education had also come into being with the permissiveness and romanticism that would later surface in the Free School movement of the 1960's. Of far more importance to Reflective Inquiry was the Eight Year Study.

Much of the Reflective Inquiry position can be found in the Eight Year Study social studies program. The most significant finding was that the experimental public school students who went on to college did as well or better than students who had taken the traditional college prep courses in history and social science.[13] The Study concluded that the further a school's curriculum varied from the conventional separate-subject curriculum, the better the students appeared to achieve. Such a finding was a powerful boost to the Reflective Inquiry position.

During this period, the professional historian and social scientist, horrified by the progressive trend, made another effort to influence the curriculum and perhaps regain a degree of self-respect. The American Historical Association, recommending that "social scientists join with educators to build a unified social studies program,"[14] created the Commission on the Social Studies in the Schools which met in 1929 and was discussed in Chapter III.

The Commission boasted some of the most eminent social scientists and educators and seemed to promise real hope for alleviating the conflicts between these two groups. The Commission report filled seventeen volumes of comprehensive analysis of the high school curriculum and included suggestions for revision. And while their conclusion, as Henry Johnson put it, proved "too brief to be always clear, too dynamic to be always free from an appearance of dogmatism far from intentional, and too general to reveal the extended analysis on which they were based."[15] the Commission did strongly endorse along with social science knowledge, the importance of teaching inquiry skills and emphasizing contemporary problems.

While the Commission on the Social Studies provided the field with the most significant examination ever undertaken, it failed to provide public schools with a recommended curricular model. The unfortunate result was even more confusion. Public schools continued to talk about "life adjustment" and inquiry, but a variety of surveys and studies conducted during the 1930's, 1940's, and 1950's demonstrated that teachers were "teaching facts and subject matter and (showing) no marked success in that area either."[16] It seemed that as educators, social scientists and school curriculum committees were holding conferences, arguing and making recommendations, public school teachers were quietly going their own way, continuing to teach subject content. While innovations and recommendations were being made, few seemed concerned with the task of re-educating teachers in the use of inquiry as a teaching method. Public school teachers continued to teach their classes as their university professors had earlier taught them.

During the 1950's and 60's, a number of social studies educators once again proposed the Reflective Inquiry position and attempted to conceptualize a powerful set of new curricular models. Growing out of the work of a number of influential philosophers and educators at Ohio State University, Maurice

109

P. Hunt and Lawrence E. Metcalf proposed a model for social studies based on teaching students inquiry skills in order to increase the proficiency and effectiveness of students' decision-making ability.[17] In advancing this proposal, Hunt and Metcalf make a clear distinction between the social studies and the social sciences. They perceive the social sciences as existing to expand the "frontiers of dependable knowledge" and the social studies teaching students the ability to make rational decisions on matters of social concern. The social sciences provide reliable facts, principles, and theories; the social studies utilize these data in the decision-making process.

Hunt and Metcalf feel the nature of contemporary society calls for a dramatic change from the usual, content-centered social studies program. They pointed to widespread conflict in contemporary society, rapid social change and competing political, economic, and social beliefs as factors which necessitate competent decision-making skills. They also identify the prevalence in our society of what they call "closed" or "problematic" areas, which they define as those aspects of American culture so saturated with controversy, confusion, ignorance, and conflict that they are largely closed to rational reflection. These areas include sex, patriotism, religion and morality, marriage, economics, social class, and race and minority group relations.[18] Hunt and Metcalf call for building the social studies on these problematic areas and helping students reflectively examine issues in the "problematic areas" of American culture. Their goal for social studies education was to teach students a method of rational thought which could be used to resolve attitudinal conflicts and value dilemmas, inquire into problems and investigate controversy.

In the 1960's another pair of social studies educators developed yet another model for the social studies as Reflective Inquiry. Donald Oliver and James P. Shaver developed what they called the "jurisprudential" method of studying public issues, a method of analyzing competing and conflicting values and making rational decisions.[19] These educators felt that by analyzing conflicts and making rational decisions, students were more effectively prepared to "participate in a democratic community" than through the preparation of "library or laboratory scholars in the university."[20]   Similar ideas have likewise been recommended by Shirley Engle, who emphasized decision-making as the "heart of the social studies,"[21] Fred Newmann, a colleague of Oliver and Shaver, who developed a model for social studies instruction based on analyzing public controversy,[22] and a growing body of other social studies educators.

Since the 1916 Committee first conceptualized the Reflective Inquiry position, it has existed primarily as a theoretical idea. Teachers and public school curriculum committees seemed to have acknowledged the idea of Reflective Inquiry, but were never able to operationalize the abstraction. This can be explained in a number of ways. The concept of Reflective Inquiry was not clearly developed initially, and teachers were never helped to learn the teaching skills associated with this approach to the social studies. As a result, teachers relied on their college professors both as teaching models and content resources. Only since the mid-1950's has the Reflective Inquiry position been developed as a practical classroom method. But once again, when compared to the extensive development in the social science area, Reflective Inquiry can point to only a few significant ventures. Such specific teaching models have been developed by Hunt and Metcalf, Oliver and Shaver, and Newmann. The Reflective Inquiry concept has also been operationalized in commercial teaching materials such as the American Educational Press, Public Issues Series/Harvard Social Studies Project,[23] Synopsis, and The Analysis of Public Issues Program[24] by Shaver and Larkins.

Reflective Inquiry: Purpose

Reflective Inquiry advocates are in agreement that the major purpose of the social studies is the enhancement of the students' decision-making abilities, for decision-making is the most important requirement of citizenship in a political democracy. The citizen, defined as a decision-maker, is one, who, having identified a problem, is able to respond to it in as rational a manner as possible. He is sensitive to the need to employ reliable data and to reflect deliberately rather than to act impulsively or from ingrained and rigid habit. The need for rational decision-making also assumes that unless a person can make satisfactory choices, he will be torn by internalized value conflict. The final assumption is that unless an entire body politic is skilled at this process, group conflict will become more and more vicious and divisive.

Although there is currently some debate among proponents of this position regarding the relationship of the social studies and democracy, there is general consensus that social studies has developed largely because of the unique aspects of our political framework.[25]   Given the assumption that decisions are supposed to be made by those who are governed, either directly or indirectly through their elected representatives, democracy requires an ability to engage fruitfully in the process of decision-making.   If we were basically an authoritarian state, with decisions made by a monarch or dictator or by an oligarchy (a group of elitist rulers), there would be no practical value in training the young in decision-making.   However, because we proclaim the values of self-rule, it is incumbent upon the culture, through its educational system, to train its citizenry in the meaning of self-rule defined as decision-making.

Reflective Inquiry: Content Defined as Social Needs

The content of social studies, as defined by advocates of the Reflective Inquiry position, consists of problems that are both personally sensed and socially shared. The assumption is that any individual problem reflects a social issue; or to put it another way, if there is a social problem, sooner or later it will affect individuals.   Thus, not only is the abuse of drugs a problem in our society, but a student in a class may be hooked on illicitly acquired amphetamines, her mother may be addicted to barbiturates, largely as the result of her physician's prescription, her dad consumes 14 cups of coffee and three packs of cigarettes each day, and her nice old grandmother has been quietly sipping a patent medicine loaded with alcohol. Not only is there a pervasive social issue called the "generation gap," but there are numerous instances in which particular parents haven't the foggiest idea what their children are talking about or how they are thinking. Not only is inflation a social problem (as this text is written) but many parents cannot afford to purchase food that is adequate nutritionally. Thus, the dichtomy between

112

"individual" and "social" is misleading. The content of the social studies defined as Reflective Inquiry consists of problems which are perceived by individuals and which also constitute widespread social issues.

Why ought social problems be based on needs and interests in the first place? The answer to this lies in psychology and learning theory employed by Reflective Inqiiry advocates. The process of inquiry, it is held, does not begin until someone has something to inquire about, a reason for thinking. The "reason for thinking" is another term for *problem*. Problems are defined as an unclear confronting situation, something that acts as a barrier to a perceived goal.

A problem may involve a *disharmony* or a *conflict*. That is, a person holds two beliefs that are contradictory. If you will look for a moment at the introduction to this chapter, you will see the teacher dealing with his students' unharmonious beliefs. One student may believe that the need of individuals to be free from meddling and surveillance by a government or employers is supremely important. Another may hold just the opposite, that the right of a government to protect itself from potential subversion or political threat takes precedence over individual liberties. It often happens that a given person holds *both* beliefs. He recognizes the claims of both values but is unable to decide which takes precedence. An individual caught on the horns of an unresolved conflict is apt to be continually uneasy and is unlikely ever to follow through a course of action without crippling hesitation, self-doubt, or guilt.

Another kind of problem involves *lack of needed information*. As we go about trying to solve our present energy crisis, there are a host of unanswered questions. What is the effect of an Alaskan pipeline on animals in that area? What is the danger of radiation from atomic fission? Do automobile engines which require combustion necessarily involve the kind of treatment which results in poor mileage (precisely the case now with the Wankel engine, the most popular candidate to replace the enormously wasteful and messy internal combustion engine)? One can also ask, in fact, is marijuana harmless as some contend, or does it really predispose to psychotic episodes, as others suggest--or, to complicate matters even further, is marijuana as carcinogenic (cancer causing) as tobacco? There are a host of questions such as these for which a good deal of important data are absent. Not only does public policy await the adequate answers to these questions, but, as we indicated above, individuals also need reliable information before they can reach solutions with which they can live.[26]

The content of the Reflective Inquiry position is based on and organized around the "needs and interests" of youth. But to say that is only to rip open an old wound and subject one's self to all the doubt, confusion and misunderstanding that have existed for the last 70 years. Most everyone can understand the "goal of Reflective Inquiry," and may, after considering the three social studies positions, even claim to support those goals. Yet when pushed on the point, almost no one can come up with an adequate explanation of how one organizes a course around such a concept as needs and interests.

To begin with, it is easier to say what a Reflective Inquiry course organized around needs and interests *is not*. It is not a course consisting of what adults think kids need: "You need this course to get into college" or "Some day you will realize how important this course is." It is likewise not a course built around the transient needs and interests of kids: "Today let's talk about choosing an acceptable mate or marriage partner" or "How many in the class are against American military involvement in 'liberation' movements in foreign countries?" It is not a course built around current events; neither is it a study of major social problems. It is not a "Hey-what-do-you-want-to-rap-about-today, do-your-own-thing" kind of course.

In order to organize a course around Reflective Inquiry, the "needs and interests" of the students must be identified and developed. But this is no easy task. In fact, it may well be one of the most difficult tasks a teacher can face. It involves developing an atmosphere of "community" in a classroom, an atmosphere of mutual respect and trust between a teacher and the students. It involves getting to know students, to understand their socio-economic background, their life-styles and life goals; it involves identifying the internal conflicts, prejudices and inconsistencies in young people. Teachers must work to help their students identify what is in their best interest to learn; what they want to do with their life and what they need in order to do it. It involves pushing students to think about what kind of person they want to become and in what kind of world they want to live.

It means helping students develop educational goals for themselves and then assisting them in developing an understanding of what they need for reaching their goals. All of this demands a personal, almost therapeutic, counseling approach of highly individualized learning. Thus, a course cannot be completely planned in advance for an entire semester or a year, for the content of the course emerges as the teacher and the students interact together. This is not to say the course is not a substantial learning experience with clearly defined, even behaviorally defined, learning objectives.

It is almost impossible to find such a course in use in public schools. There are, however, some outstanding examples. The St. Paul Open School, and optional public school, has a K-12 curriculum with no required courses. Learning is completely individualized, and the key to each student's development is a learning counselor. The counselor is both a "gadfly" and a "midwife," working with students to develop their "needs" and then creating ways to meet those needs. Students may be fulfilling their "needs" through independent study, projects, social experiences, and internships in the community, or by taking short, single-focus mini-courses. The learning counselor orchestrates the learning experience by carefully developing and monitoring personal learning contracts with each student. Similar social studies programs are found at the Walden III School in Racine, Wisconsin; Pioneer II in Ann Arbor; and a growing number of what have been referred to as "optional public schools."

Recently, one of the authors was visiting the class of a highly successful Reflective Inquiry teacher, and her experiences should prove useful in understanding the "needs and interests" organization. Teaching in rural, Southern Indiana schools, most of her students were poor, often referred to as "Stoneys" since their parents usually worked in the limestone quarries of Southern Indiana. Many experienced substantial reading difficulties. The students were not avid learners; they were absent much of the time, and when they turned 16, they usually drop-

115

ped out of school, thus perpetuating the poverty cycle in their area..

The teacher started the school year by holding informal discussions with her students, telling them about herself and asking about their own lives. She asked them to write stories about themselves and for those who had difficulty writing, she had them tape record their words. She used a number of value clarification strategies to encourage students to reflect on their life. Soon, she had begun to develop strong rapport with her students. Throughout this period, she learned a good deal about her students. They inevitably were in trouble with the local police, many were already on probation, and some of their older brothers and sisters were in prison. Most all of the girls got pregnant young and were forced to marry, subsequently rearing rather large families. Almost all planned to stay in the area and most planned to work in the quarries. When the teacher first raised questions concerning the students' lives. they could not understand what she was asking. Most of them had never imagined that they so much as possessed the freedom to "do" something with their lives; most simply accepted what was supposed to and usually did occur.

Because hassles with the police were such a significant aspect of their lives, the teacher initiated a unit she called "Law and Order." She talked with the students about juvenile crime, pushing them to try and think about the implications. To get the class involved and motivated, she invited two local policemen as guest speakers in the class. The discussion that day was excellent. Many students got angry at what the policemen had to say but all were interested. The discussion the next several days centered on helping students to identify what they thought were important issues and questions and then to develop a list of other speakers. The students suggested the probation officer, the juvenile judge, and two students already serving probated sentences in the class volunteered to tell the class about their experiences. One student's older brother, who had served time in a reformatory, also spoke to the class. Later the class visited the local Juvenile Court and the County Jail and even planned and carried out a field trip to the State Reformatory. Through-out it all, the students were clarifying their

116

own ideas and values, learning their constitutional rights and reflecting on whether or not they wished to end up in the reformatory or prison. Later the class explored varieties of career possibilities, everything from factory worker to fireman, to postman, and even career soldier. They studied birth control and family planning and units entitled "How to Live Cheaply" and "Alternative Life Styles." Throughout the course, students were pushed to reflect on who they were and who they wanted to become; what they were doing with their life and what they wanted to do with it. Did they want to break the poverty cycle, and if so, how could they do it?

A similiar example can be found in Jonathan Kozol's book *Free Schools.* Kozol attacks the idea of letting kids "do-their-own-thing," especially if they are black, inner-city kids, who are deep in poverty and cannot read or do basic arithmetic. For such students to have a curriculum based on "rap session," macramé, and rock music, Kozol argues, is to inflict upon them a savage wrong. He believes students should be confronted with exploring what they "need" to survive in the urban area. He urges that schools work rigorously to teach these "survival skills" which might include everything from basic reading and mathematics to political efficiency.

In each of the above examples, the teacher was working to develop rigorous, substantial learning experiences that grew out of the deepest, most intimate needs of students. This is what has been meant by those calling for Reflective Inquiry, but it is also the kind of meaningful learning that has seldom been seen in public schools. Let us now turn to an analysis of what was just called "the Reflective Inquiry process."

Reflective Inquiry: Method Defined as Reflective Process

The teaching process just described flows from a set of beliefs about how thought takes place. John Dewey, who conceptualized this process at the turn of the century, gave a good deal of credit for his analysis to Charles S. Peirce, a somewhat eccentric logician and scientist who attempted to identify the characteristics of scientific thinking. As we discuss what is called "the Reflective process," "the stages of inquiry," or "the implications of the scientific method," please keep the following in mind: although we discuss these stages as if they were separate, in reality they are not. That stage we call "uncertainty and doubt" may reoccur throughout. Hypothesizing does not appear only once: individuals try out various hypotheses at many stages. The entire thinking process is jumbled and hesitating as sudden flashes of insight and intuition alternate with long dry spells where nothing much may seem to happen. The conceptual schema we now present, therefore, must be seen as a theoretical description. It does not adequately describe the reality. In the following pages we will attempt to describe and illustrate the Reflective Inquiry process, explore the techniques of classroom discussion so important to a productive inquiry, and finally illustrate the ways teachers may grade and evaluate students' inquiry performance.

A. The Process of Reflective Inquiry

1. *Experience.* The process of inquiry begins with an experience, any interaction between a person and his environment. The experience transforms a settled and untroubled situation into a confused and uncertain one. An event--or, as is quite often true, a recollection of an event--forces the person into an "I don't know" situation. Something has happened or has been thought of which cannot be assimilated into a person's stock of belief and knowledge.

An individual may behave in a way which is unexpected. A question may be raised which casts doubt upon an already accepted explanation. A situation arises whose ambiguity is so marked, that an individual does not know what to make of it. An often used sentence to describe a problem is "An event in which the situation and its meaning are not clear." As one goes about his normal life, such situations constantly occur again and again. In a classroom learning situation, the teacher may have to carefully organize "encounter experiences," the areas of studied needs and interests, that create the uneasiness ending, hopefully, in reflection.

2. *Doubt and Uncertainty.* There follows a period of doubt and uncertainty. A kind of tension arises in the person as his perception of the experience leaves him uneasy, troubled, puzzled. For Reflective Inquirers this stage is essential. They argue that

it is pointless to ask someone to think without a problem for thinking is defined as that process which is designed to remove a problem. It goes without saying that all of us try to avoid or evade a problem: we deny, we rationalize, we simply refuse to deal with or confront the situation. This is precisely why one of the major tasks of a Reflective Inquiry teacher--a task that is largely an art--is perhaps the most important aspect of his job. The Reflective Inquiry teacher uses any way he can to generate a "sense of problem," i.e., a feeling of doubt or uncertainty, the motivation that will lead students to begin to think.

3. *Framing the Problem.* To begin the process of handling one's doubt, one attempts to frame the problem, that is, to create a statement of the problem. The statement of the problem describes the boundaries within which the conflict is seen and the tension created. The reason for this is that it is impossible to explore every aspect of a complex and unclear situation simultaneously. Therefore, different elements of the problem are marked off from each other. And therefore, a person begins to take stock--that is, to assess both the situation and his understanding of the situation. To do this, an individual begins to ask himself a series of questions. These questions include:

a. What do I know? That is, what knowledge am I fairly sure I possess?

b. What do I *think* I know? That is, in essence, a matter of examining one's own assumptions. One begins to make a distinction between what he is fairly sure he knows and what he believes to be true.

c. What do I not know? Often placing a line between what is known and what is unknown is an important prerequisite to solving a problem. By simply identifying and naming the unknown elements, one can at least begin to define the nature of the problem.

d. What do I understand? That is, having identified the boundaries that frame the problem, one questions whether or not these boundaries make sense.

4. *Formulating Hypotheses.* When framing hypotheses one is literally "brainstorming the possibilities." The framing of the problem establishes limits within which to hypothesize. An

119

hypothesis is an attempt at using the known to suggest explanations of the unknown. In other words, following an experience which generates doubt, a problem is framed which contains within it conflicting ideas. With this frame of reference one suggests hypotheses that function as proposed explanations which, if valid, will resolve the doubt or conflict.

5. *Exploring and Evidencing.* The title of this stage is almost self-explanatory. This is the stage of gathering and evaluating sources of evidence. This stage includes demonstration of the validity or invalidity of hypotheses. It involves exploring many possible sources of information, then gathering data to be used as evidence in evaluating the original hypothesis.

6. *Generalization.* The final step in the inquiry process is generalization. The generalization is a statement about how well the hypotheses have helped to clarify or resolve the problem. Clearly the generalization is more than a mere restating of an hypothesis but rather a statement of how the hypothesis provides an explanation of the problem. Do you recall in Step 3 (Framing the Problem?) the example of how one defines a problem? There were four categories starting with (a) What I know, and ending with (d) What I think I understand? A generalization provides continuity and explains the relationship between the four question categories of the problem. Generalizations are "tentative" knowledge which may assist one in refining the original statement of the problem.

The term "tentative" is used to show that the knowledge gained through exploration and evidencing is qualified by the assumptions one makes. Clearly the task now, if one were to continue inquiring into an issue, is to investigate further into dimensions of the problem which probably would lead to new questions and new hypotheses. Also, it is entirely possible that because one might reframe the problem one may seek sources of evidence which might not have seemed appropriate before. Very simply, what we are saying is that inquiry leads us through a process of identifying, defining, and finally refining. Knowledge is only as *"good"* as the assumption made.

At the beginning of this chapter you saw an example of a problem typically selected by social studies teachers who advocate Reflective Inquiry. The problem involved a contradiction, a disharmony, that exists both in our society and reflects itself in the attitudes of individual members. The teacher, you will recall, encouraged students to express their feelings and after getting the known facts straight, helped students define the conflict: in this case, the desire for privacy and protection from snooping as it conflicts with the need for the government to protect itself from internal subversion. Let us look at another example of Reflective Inquiry.

Problems selected by Reflective Inquiry advocates differ in important ways from those of Social Scientists or Citizenship Transmission proponents. Social Scientists select those problems which have already been entertained by their colleagues. Citezenship Transmitters choose problems which are traditionally conceived and are expressed as questions that have established answers. However, as we have seen, the Reflective Inquiry teacher must select an issue that students identify as a problem. He knows that a viable problem exists when his students differ sharply among themselves. In the following hypothetical situation, an 11th grade civics class, the teacher is considering the topic of taxation, ordinarily a prelude to suffocating boredom. But in this example, the teacher is a Reflective Inquirer, and through close association with his students and through careful development, he has identified an area of student "needs and interests" that he sets out to explore reflectively.

B. Illustrating the Method

1. The Encounter Experience

"What percentage of our total taxes is spent for welfare?" he asks.

Without answering this question, a student volunteers, "We're spending too much tax money, and most of it is going to support a bunch of welfare bums who are too shiftless and lazy to support themselves."

"Well, all right. Just how much of your tax dollar is spent for welfare services?"

No one answers, for in fact, the students lack information. However, this does not prevent anyone from having a definite opinion. "I don't know what it is, but too much is being spent. I

121

agree with Earl." The teacher will get back to this question later, but he senses that something important is happening. He decides to probe a bit more.

"What welfare bums are you talking about? Where?"

"Right here in this city," Harold answers, not really specifying a population as the teacher requested.

Nancy begins to entertain doubts about Harold's knowledge

"Oh, Harold, you just don't know what you are talking about."

Before Harold can snarl back, the teacher steps in and tries to calm the frayed nerves that the topic immediately lays bare. "Now, let's not engage in *ad hominen* arguments. Remember, we talked about this a while ago. Let's confine ourselves to the topic. I'm not sure, however, what the topic is. Is it taxation or welfare?"

2. Generating Doubt and Uncertainty

The question sinks in after a few moments, and John replies, "It's both. You know, welfare bums are paid from taxation."

"Okay. Does the federal government pay for welfare? The state government? The local government?

No answer. After a while Earl says, with some hesitation, "I think it's local. There's a food stamp center downtown."

"That's a federal program, you dummy," Frank says encouragingly.

"So," the teacher asks once again, "is welfare federal, state, or local?"

There is no consensus, but the question, which highlights the extent of misunderstanding and misinformation, does not dampen emotion.

John, whose parents are educated and affluent, decides to add another interpretation. "My father says that every generation always has its poor and that these poor stay on the bottom until eventually they rise."

"Rise where?" the teacher asks.

"You know. Rise," John says, as if poverty were a self-evident phenomenon and everyone knew what "rise" meant. Indeed, everyone does know that "rise" means to go up in socioeconomic rank, but since the topic of social class is generally a taboo subject in social studies classrooms, students' knowledge of the facts of social stratification are as fuzzy as their knowledge of poverty and welfare. However, enough progress has been made for the teacher to attempt a summary:

"Somehow we have linked poverty, welfare, and taxation. Does anyone care to tell us what the essential problem is?"

Again silence. Students investigate their pencils and shift uncomfortably in their seats. Finally Nancy states the following: "I think the problem is that some of us," she glares at Harold, "just don't want to help out the poor."

Harold rises to the occasion. "You mean help out the niggers, don't you, Nancy?"

The class waits for the teacher to respond. The two Black students in class turn to focus angry stares at Harold, but do not afford him the satisfaction of responding to his epithet. The teacher thinks to himself, "Social class, poverty, taxation, and now race. Now what?"

3. Framing the Problem

Up to this point, some necessary behaviors have occurred. Students have felt, or perhaps been made to feel, a sense of problem. Emotions run high, irrationality abounds, values clash, and the misinformation and misunderstanding are abundantly evident. But these are essential--that is, they are the behaviors which necessarily signal the presence of a problem. The inquiry process begins, it does not end at this point.

What must now happen is for some focusing to take place. Another way of saying "focusing" is to talk about framing the problem, i.e., students sense that some ideas must be excluded and some included. A colleague puts it colloquially: "You have to build a fence around the barn." The reason for the fence, the problem framework, is simple: it is not possible to address oneself to everything at once; therefore one has to decide what elements of a problem he will attend to.

In the situation just described, the teacher and his students may frame a problem in terms of racial prejudice, social welfare, poverty, taxes, etc. The teacher might focus on the racial slur used by the student and question why the poor are often sterotyped and ridiculed. Such a line of questioning might "frame-off" the problem from issues of taxation and welfare. If on the other hand, the teacher and the students feel strongly their need to sort out their confusion about welfare, they may focus on the following problem: Why is there such widespread poverty in the United States? But in order to explore this question, a welter of questions almost inevitably arise: What is poverty? How is it defined and by whom? Is poverty a statistical concept? Is it a culture (that is, the "culture of poverty" concept)? How many poor are there? How many poor are there in this country, as opposed to other countries? What is the demographic distribution of the poor?

Other questions are legitimate, of course, but questions like these will at least need to be asked, or the topic will forever stay at the diffuse and incoherent level where it began.

The alert teacher will also want to see his class frame questions about race. Some questions are: What is race? Is "race" the same as "class?" Is it the same as "culture?" Where are races? What is the statistical relationship between race and poverty in this culture? Is the relationship other than statistical, that is, can one posit a cause-and-effect relationship? If so, how is this relationship known?

Questions relating to taxation and welfare might include: How much is spent on "welfare?" What is defined as welfare? What proportion of all taxation is spent on welfare? From what sources? Is this country's welfare program adequate? How much of our welfare spending is waste and how is this known? To what extent is our welfare program meeting the people's needs, and, if this is granted, what needs? Who is proposing what kinds of improvements in welfare? What accounts for our society's inability to make basic changes in its welfare structure?

In framing the above problem, students have had time to think about all of these questions and to use their existing knowledge (what they know or think they know and what they think they understand) and finally begin to identify what they do not know. Almost immediately the class runs into trouble as was obvious, for students cannot so much as agree on a definition of poverty. The class finally concludes that poverty comprises that section of the population which makes less than $4,000 per year. As the inquiry gets underway, they will return to lower or raise this figure and also change their initial definition of poverty. At the outset of the discussion, the class agrees--even the Black students--that those in poverty are predominantly Black. Only later as they begin to study poverty among the "aged," will they return to correct this misconception.

4. Hypothesizing

As we explained earlier, an hypothesis is a statement which is designed ultimately to explain and to predict and which therefore requires vigorous testing. Students are encouraged to reflect on the problem they have identified. If the students in the illustration above choose to focus on the problem of poverty, the teacher would attempt to get his students brainstorming as many possible ideas, i.e., hypotheses, as they could. He would not evaluate these ideas, and would never say to the students, "No, that's not a good hypothesis," but rather he would attempt to get as many possible--even conflicting--explanations to the problem. He continually pushes students to clarify ideas and then writes them on the board, asking, "Is this what you mean?" Again and again he summarizes what has been said and asks, "Can you think of any other ideas?" After the discussion has slowed and it seems they have exhausted their flow of ideas, the teacher attempts to get even more ideas. He may ask, "What do you think Archie Bunker would say, or perhaps Jimmy Carter or Caesar Chavez?" Once again the class may be stimulated to "think" of other possible hypotheses. Finally, the chalk board is filled with hypotheses that the class hopes or believes will resolve their problem. The following are sample hypotheses taken from their list:
1. Certain ethnic groups are naturally lazy and refuse to work.
2. Certain ethnic groups are naturally less intelligent and genetically inferior.
3. Certain ethnic groups are discriminated against because of poverty.
4. The existing welfare system perpetuates the poverty cycle by rewarding those who will not work.

The teacher then begins talking to the students about where they can go to find information concerning the hypotheses and what kinds of information are needed. To help the students focus on their collection of data, the teacher helps the class translate these hypotheses into "if-then" statements, i.e., *If certain ethnic groups are naturally lazy and refuse to work, then* what would we expect to find? Such a discussion begins to push the students to think of ways to test their ideas.

5. *Exploring and Evidencing*

Evidence is not merely information; evidence is analogous to the term "clue." Whatever one needs to solve a problem is relevant evidence. If one wishes a simple analogy, think of stones lying on the ground. These are "information." The same stones, gathered deliberately and consciously used to form a house or a fence, now constitute "evidence."

Whereas the Social Scientist tends to confine his evidence to that which is accepted conventionally by his colleagues, the Reflective Inquirer tends to gather a much wider range of evidence--concepts, facts, theories, and findings taken from all of the social science disciplines, and going beyond, often including literature, psychoanalysis, psychiatry, and jurisprudence. Whereas the Citizenship Transmission teacher tends to confine himself to concepts specifically mentioned in his textbook, teacher guide, or syllabus, the Reflective Inquiry advocate is quite satisfied to use student experiences and their interpretations--as well as more formally acquired information. The idea is *not* to separate facts from values and immature student expressions from sophisticated theories. The idea is to encourage expression of preference, but to insist upon analysis, to demand that everybody's contribution be analyzed carefully--including that of the teacher, for he is not *above* the process--he is part of the process.

The purpose of analysis involves the seeking and testing of meaning. Questions that are continually raised are: What does this mean? What does it not mean? Is it relevant? What is the status of this knowledge--is it known intuitively, is it the commonly held position, the "conventional wisdom," to use John Kenneth Galbraith's term? Can one interpret this concept differently? Why does one assert this? Do others assert the opposite, and if so, why? What would happen if this were true? What assumptions are being made now? What assumptions must be made?

126

Note the character of these questions. They are not simple ones that can be answered in a few words. They require facts to be answered. All interpretations depend upon certain assumptions about values and these assumptions should be made explicit. Much of the analysis needed to deal with these questions will be borrowed from Social Scientists, as indeed, much of the data will come from findings of Social Scientists. But by no means all. Richard Wright's *Black Boy* and James Baldwin's *The Fire Next Time* are as relevant to these questions as are Professor Moynihan's tax reform proposals.

Although a fair number of teachers have expressed the view that inquiry is a matter of a pleasantly heated exchange of opinion unsupported by any facts, nothing could be further from the truth. The gathering and analysis of facts is essential to the proper conduct of inquiry. The difficulty is that Reflective Inquirers advocate a distinctively different use of facts: the facts are not learned from a textbook and memorized by students who are tested on them later. Rather, the facts are gathered by students from many sources and used to determine the validity of different points of view.

From what sources? Textbooks are, of course, not prohibited. If used, however, they are used selectively: not read word for word, but consulted as one source of data. The teacher is also not prohibited from dispensing facts. However, the teacher's lecture is not the major source of information.[27] The teacher may lecture when some information is needed immediately. He may also interpret some complex ideas, as for instance, providing a brief explanation of the genetics of racial inheritance, the meaning of the GNP, or the significance of Moynihan's welfare reform proposals. However, the teacher's interpretations are neither exclusive nor dominant.

Reflective Inquiry teachers cultivate sources of information the way prize dahlia growers dote over their flowers. Some of them have persuaded their schools to purchase subscriptions to newspapers and journals, which are then often kept in classrooms. Others make a deal with friends: instead of throwing away copies of their journals, they give them to the social studies teachers who will, in turn, see that their students use them. Some teachers keep an article file in their room and maintain folders full of journal and newspaper articles on a variety of topics.

Some teachers encourage their students to interview and record information from knowledgeable persons in the community or from specialists in a variety of areas. Some teachers have acquired the knack of getting free information from industries and special interest groups which love to send schools their version of reality. Many have open pipelines to university professors whom they tap regularly for ideas and interpretations on matters that touch upon the province of sociology, anthropology, history, political science, economics, geography, and psychology.

The various libraries--schools, public, or adjacent university-- are all fair game for the inquiry teacher. Students are taught to locate information in libraries, to take notes, and to organize and arrange their information in careful and accurate fashion. The encyclopedia, like the textbook, is not forgotten, but in addition, students are encouraged and trained to use monographs, specialized collections, government reports, oral interviews, and other sources of information not usually considered appropriate for high school students. The practice of introducing a "unit" on using the library and writing reports is excluded deliberately. The gathering of information is not something to be taught in one section of the course and then forgotten. It is an essential part of the process of inquiry and is taught and practiced over and over again, throughout the course.

6. *Generalization*

After the sources of information have been identified, and the data has been gathered, organized, and interpreted, some of the hypotheses will have been synthesized. Others have been called into question and new hypotheses will have been generated and tested. In the end, the teacher and his students will conclude their investigation by developing a number of generalizations. These generalizations consist of the "knowledge" they have developed. In the example above, the students might conclude their inquiry into the "reasons for widespread poverty in the United States," by generalizing that:

1. The poor in America are usually composed of the elderly, the unskilled, and ethnic minorities.

2. Much poverty in America seems to be perpetuated by cultural and institutional racism.

3. Most welfare programs that have been used (welfare payments, food stamps, vocational training, etc.) have proven to be only expedient, "stop-gap" responses and offer no comprehensive solutions.

You will notice that the final generalizations are far more sophisticated than the earlier hypotheses, reflecting the insights the students have gained during their study. But the students realize that these generalizations are only "tentative" and could be called into question by later inquiries and new knowledge. Besides the generalizations, the students have gained a wealth of knowledge. The have learned accurate conceptual definitions of poverty, welfare, racism, and more. They have clarified their own values, and may have even eliminated some of their own prejudices and biases. They are also well informed in the working of a number of our federal programs.

C. Classroom Discussion: The Heart of the Matter

The heart of the inquiry process is classroom discussion. By discussion is not meant a conventional recitation or bull session.[28] A recitation is simply a rehashing of information gained from textbooks and lectures. The purpose of a recitation is to "fix" the information in students' minds. A bull session is a heated exchange of opinion, unsupported by formal considerations of criteria, evidence, or logic. A discussion involves a disciplined exchange of ideas in which the central purpose is that students clarify their belief structure. The discussions which Reflective Inquiry teachers conduct are designed specifically to assist students to think in ways which are more harmonious and consistent with available evidence.

Some part of the discussion is devoted to finding out the facts: who said what, where, and what does it mean? With regard to our original question concerning poverty, welfare, taxation, and class, here are some examples: What is the official governmental definition of poverty? Who thought up this definition? How is it different from the idea that poverty is not a matter of a fixed income but of culture? What is the anthropologist's definition of race? What problems are there in any definition of race? What data are there concerning race and income? What limitations are there in the interpretation of such data? Who is eligible for county welfare? What proportion of this county's expenditures are devoted to welfare? Who actually disburses welfare payments? According to what criteria?

Another set of questions concern the wider context. That is, in what context is the problem to be interpreted, and related to this, what do social scientists say about the problem? Examples of this kind of question are: Why, according to some sociologists, do middle class Americans so resent welfare claimants? What is there about the Protestant Ethic and the American dream[29] that intensify this resentment? What evidence is there that government subsidies will inevitably blunt the desire to work?

Yet another set of questions is designed to elicit evaluations from students. Examples are: How do you feel about the Guaranteed Annual Income? What is your reaction to the proposal that all welfare requirements should be tightened? What do you think will happen to an unemployable welfare mother who is tossed off welfare? How humanitarian is a particular proposal? How would you evaluate the belief that welfare simply subsidizes sexual promiscuity? Is it fair that our society does not mind subsidizing the middle class but does resent subsidizing the poor?

Please understand that these three types of questions are not asked separately, in isolation from each other. Many different types of questions are interspersed throughout the discussion. Some of them are factual and may be followed by evaluative responses.

D. Classroom Evaluation: A Different Conception

An important part of the Reflective Inquiry unit is evaluation. The basic purpose of evaluation is to ask the question, Did my students actually learn what they should have learned? If I have specified to myself clearly enough what they should have learned, how do I go about discovering this? The task is to have decided what was to be learned, and to devise some means of informing both student and teacher what was learned, to what extent and by whom. Evaluation, as such, is not a matter of giving one a paper and pencil test at the end of a predetermined time. Nor is it a matter of devising long lists of objective questions.

Evaluation occurs at many discrete points in a reflective unit. In fact, the teacher is constantly gaining feedback on his students--by listening to them, by analyzing what is apparently learned, what is still unclear, what is sensed, and what is articulated in verbal form. The inquiry teacher is concerned not only with cognitive growth but also attitudinal change. Thus he is constantly discovering what beliefs, values, attitudes, and feelings are expressed by his students, how they are expressed and what they mean.

Since the conventional essay--and most particularly the objective test--is based upon assumptions that he does not accept, the Reflective Inquiry teacher needs to find other instruments.[30] Therefore, he tends to use a variety of different instruments, some of which may involve problem-centered essay questions, some of which may involve the performance of certain skills, some of which may be done by one person, and some by a group. Here are some examples:

1. A set of essay questions, to be taken home and answered by all students, which might be phrased as follows:

a). React to this statement, "The poor are poor because they have learned to be poor and transmit poverty to their children. The cure for poverty lies in education."

b). If there is no demonstrated scientific connection between race and poverty, why are Indians poor?

2. A group of students are to present their findings, in a panel, to the entire class. They will be evaluated on the thoroughness of their research, their demonstrated ability to synthesize their facts, their clarity of presentation, and their ability to analyze their findings.

3. A number of students were asked to identify agencies in their town which deal with poverty. Individuals from these agencies were interviewed on tape. The tapes were presented to the class, were commented upon by these students, who then answered a variety of questions

put to them by class members.

4. A number of other students were asked to put together statistics, gathered from federal, state, and local sources, and after conferring with an economist, were to summarize their interpretations in a handout. The handout was then dittoed and passed out to all students.

5. After having researched case studies, a few students were asked to devise a playlet, illustrating salient aspects of poverty. These playlets were then followed by impromptu sociodramas and then a classroom discussion.

6. One very able student was asked to read Sanchez' *Children of Poverty*. Another student, equally able, was asked to read Myrdal's *Chinese Village*. Both then presented their reactions to the class, which then discussed the difference between poverty among Puerto Ricans in New York and poverty in China.

If the reader is now thinking to himself, "Well. That's funny. These 'evaluation instruments' are also teaching strategies," he is entirely correct. An evaluation device in a Reflective Inquiry classroom has a twofold purpose: it provides an opportunity for learning as well as a means of gaining feedback.

One final point: it may be that the teacher is ultimately going to be stuck with an A,B,C,D,F scale, and while this is to some extent unfortunate, it appears to be impossible to eliminate. However, even though there are enormous philosophical problems inherent in a unilinear scale marked off at discrete points, the Reflective teacher recognizes that such is a cultural bias which he probably cannot change. However, while he must decide who gets an A and who a B, he is also trying to refine and elaborate his own criteria. Unlike other teachers who ask themselves only, How frequently did the child's answers agree with mine--the correct ones?--the Reflective Inquiry teacher must pay attention to an entire *process*. Thus, as this teacher gains more experience teaching, and more knowledge of what goes into the inquiry process, he pays more attention to many, many aspects of a student's cognitive and affective growth.

Critical Evaluation

The most salient criticism that can be made of the Reflective Inquiry position is that its highly abstract nature renders it much less clear and understandable than the other two. The Social Science position, although supported by complex and abstract theory, has generated a good many curriculum units which come equipped with outlines, syllabi, hints, multi-media materials, and lesson plans. The Citizenship Transmission tradition, because it is the most pervasive and easily demonstrated, is rather easy for teachers to use. However, partly because of the philosophical depth, the lack of systematic explanation, and the paucity of curriculum materials, most teachers have only learned the *language* of Reflective Inquiry-- problems, problem-solving, decision-making, citizenship, etc.-- and cannot translate these terms into teaching behavior.

John Dewey's attempt--during the last five years of the 19th Century and the first 50 years of this one--to develop Reflective Inquiry theory has provided almost insoluble problems. First, by the very nature of his philosophy, which avoided most of the conventional philosophical positions, Dewey made it difficult for most of his followers to assimilate his ideas. Second, even his loyal followers were not able to agree on some basic points.[31] Third, while there are some articulate spokesmen for the Reflective Inquiry position, there are few who have spelled out the meaning and implications for teachers. The Hunt-Metcalf social studies text attempted this, but there is reason to believe that many of the undergraduates and even graduate students who read the text did not understand it very well.

Another major criticism of the position is that it requires a good deal more from its supporters than the other two. A claimant to Reflective Inquiry must not only possess a grasp of philosophy and psychology (especially learning theory) but must also be well informed in the social sciences and must be able to lead his discussions, order and use resource materials, devise appropriate evaluative instruments, and many other things. In short, the demands made on teachers by the position is such that one can conceivably say, "If men were angels, all would be well," that is, if teachers were truly able to muster the knowledge, energy, and skill required to translate the position effectively into action, it would be workable. But, since they are manifestly not able to do so, then one can argue that the position is simply out of reach of most teachers.

It is plausible to argue that not only is the position not comprehensible to teachers, its very basic assumptions may well be wrong. Reflective Inquirers claim that by exposing students to conflict areas in the society, they are sharpening decision-making skills, promoting thought, and enhancing problem-solving abilities. This may well be so. But, one can then ask, Is teaching students to be critical of their tradition the best way to guarantee survival of that tradition? While criticism may be defined as "skilled judgement,"[32] most of us tend to equate "criticism" with "destructive criticism." It may well be that students who look deeply and carefully into the myriad religious, economic, and political conflicts may decide that the game is not worth playing, i.e., our form of society may not be as good and beneficient as we like to think it is...and that it is incapable of significant change.

It may well also be that the criticism made by Professor James Shaver that Reflective Inquiry ought to be based upon certain "fixed moral principles" means that Reflective Inquiry is really not tenable. As we stated in the final part of the chapter on Social Studies taught as Social Science, it has been held that *any* teaching stance ought to grow out of acceptance of the fundamental rights of all humans to dignity and equality. If Professor Shaver is correct, if there are certain values that are so basic, so important and fundamental, then it may well be that Reflective Inquiry is, as many of its opponents have claimed for more than a half century, untenable and destructive.

In addition to the density of the Reflective Inquiry position itself, it seems very likely that many schools simply are not organized to permit students the freedom, the opportunity, or the means to inquire. The very basic assumptions of Reflective Inquiry are essentially foreign to a school day broken into so many 50-minute periods, with subject matter disciplines carefully separated, and a host of topics declared off limits to student inquiry. Chairs bolted down in straight rows, libraries presided over by individuals who are distressed by more than three students at a time, field trips all but impossible to schedule because of logistics and liability problems, curricula often mandated either by the legislature or by State departments of public instruction--virtually every aspect of most public schools simply mitigate against the proposals of Reflective Inquiry advocates. The system, in short, cannot be challenged, or at least, it is too wearying for most teachers to do so.

Finally, the very core assumption of Reflective Inquiry--that training problem-solving is essential--may be fallacious. After all, as Dewey himself admitted,[33] most decisions are made without conscious thought. Most of the time, most of us act either through ingrained habit or rapidly, even impulsively and reflexively. If so, what then is the need for training in a mode of thinking which most of us will never use?

In short, there is ample reason to believe that the Reflective Inquiry position is too difficult, dense, abstract, and impractical to apply to the every day tasks of ordinary teachers.

Notes

[1] James L. Barth and S. Samuel Shermis, "Defining the Social Studies: An Exploration of Three Traditions," *Social Education* (see footnote 21), 37, No. 7 (November, 1970), p. 749. Other definitions can be found in John Dewey, *How We Think* (Boston: D.C. Heath and Company, 1933); Ernest E. Bayles, *Democratic Educational Theory* (New York: Harper and Brothers, Publishers, 1960); H. Gordon Hullfish and Phillip Smith, *Reflective Thinking* (New York: Dodd, Mead and Company, 1961).

[2] Neil Postman and Charles Weingartner, "A Careful Guide To The School Squabble," *Psychology Today,* VII, No. 5 (October, 1973), pp. 76-86.

[3] Neil Postman and Charles Weingartner, *Teaching As a Subversive Activity* (New York: Delacorte Press, 1969), p. 10.

[4] Alvin Toffler, *Future Shock* (New York: Random House, 1970).

[5] Allen Nevins, "The Explosive Excitement of History," *Saturday Review,* LI, No. 14 (April 6, 1968), p. 13.

[6] Alfred North Whitehead, *Adventure of Ideas* (New York: Macmillan Company, 1933), p. 117.

[7] Margaret Mead, "The Impact of Culture on Personalty Development in the United States," *Understanding the Child,* XX (January, 1951; Lancaster, PA.: National Association for Mental Health, Inc.), pp. 17-18.

[8]Marshall McLuhan and George B. Leonard, "The Future of Education: The Class of 1989," *Look,* XXXI, No. 4 (February 21, 1967), p. 25.

[9]Postman and Weingartner, *Teaching As A Subversive Activity, op. cit.,* p. 13.

[10]Robert S. Lynd, *Knowledge For What* (Princeton, New Jersey: Princeton University Press, 1939), p. 21.

[11]Henry Johnson, *Teaching of History* (New York: Macmillan Company, 1940), p. 74.

[12]"A Report of the Committee on Social Studies on the Reorganization of Secondary Education of the NEA," *National Education Bulletin,* No. 28 (Washington, D.C.: Bureau of Education, 1916).

[13]Wilford Merton Aiden, *The Story of the Eight Year Study* (New York: Harper and Brothers, 1942), pp.111-112.

[14]Erling Hunt, "Changing Perspectives in the Social Studies," *High School Social Studies Perspectives,* ed. Harold C. Hunt (Boston: Houghton-Mifflin, 1962), p. 19.

[15]Johnson, *op. cit.,* p. 78.

[16]James A. Quillen and Lavone A. Hanna, *Education for Social Competence* (Chicago: Scott-Foresman and Company, 1961), p. 15.

[17]Maurice P. Hunt and Lawrence E. Metcalf, *Teaching High School Social Studies* (2d ed. rev.; New York: Harper and Row, Publishers, 1968).

[18]*Ibid.,* p. 233.

[19]Donald Oliver and James Shaver, *Teaching Public Issues in High School* (Boston: Houghton-Mifflin Company, 1966).

[20]*Ibid.,* p. 233.

[21]Shirley H. Engle, "Decision-Making: The Heart of the Social Studies," *Social Education,* XXIV, No. 7 (November, 1960), pp. 301-304, 306.

[22]Fred Newmann, *Clarifying Public Controversy* (Boston: Little, Brown and Company, 1970).

[23]American Education Publications Unit Book, 55 High Street, Middletown, Connecticut, 06457.

[24]James P. Shaver and A. Guy Larkins, *Analysis of Public Issues: Decision-Making in a Democracy* (Boston: Houghton-Mifflin Company, 1973).

[25]Some Reflective Inquiry advocates seem to believe that the outcomes reached in a social studies class must necessarily support a political democracy. Some maintain that all outcomes reached in a class must result in some form of political action. The authors do not accept either of these two positions.

[26]Note the phrase, "with which they can live." In fact, in our society, it is difficult to formulate both public policy and individual solutions in such a manner that people can live comfortably with their decisions. No sooner do we as a society decide that equality under the law implies equal educational opportunity, than we decide that we cannot stand the idea of busing kids to schools where they can receive such an opportunity. No sooner does an individual decide that he must possess, immediately, a range of consumer products that he kicks himself for getting trapped in the installment credit trap. When Dr. Karen Horney wrote *The Neurotic Personality of Our Time,* she was not whistling Dixie. The problem, of course, has to do with a tendency not to foresee consequences. And the foreseeing of consequences is the name of the game for Reflective Inquirers.

[27]In the Citizenship Transmission tradition, the teacher is more a source of interpretation than he is of information. The teacher's interpretations are almost the heart and soul of traditional Citizenship Transmission teaching.

[28]S. Samuel Shermis and Robert Kime, "Preliminary Criteria for Distinguishing Between a Reflective Social Studies Discussion and a Conventional Recitation," an unpublished manuscript (Purdue Univesity, 1967). See also S. Samuel Shermis and James Barth, "Inquiry Without Structure: Fifty Years of Classical Progressivism," a paper delivered before the Philosophy of Education Society, San Francisco, 1972.

[29]That is, the Protestant Ethic asserts that individuals should work hard, be thrifty, and not waste time or money. Those who have not succeeded, however "success" may be defined, have failed because they did not have strength of character. The American Dream is usually phrased as a belief that one should be able to go just as far as he can, restricted only by considerations of ability and ambition.

[30]Both the conventional essay and the objective test are designed to measure the "rightness" of a student's responses. The assumption is that there are specific, correct answers which the teacher knows in advance and students are to learn. This assumption leads to testing procedures which are both too authoritarian and too simplistic for the Reflective Inquiry teacher.

[31]For instance, during the 1930's, a debate, never satisfactorily resolved, over the issue of indoctrination, was carried on in the pages of *Social Frontier*. A number of educational leaders, all claiming to be followers of Dewey, advanced different claims. Finally, in the later 1930's, Dewey himself tired of the issue and quit.

[32]Its original meaning in Greek.

[33]In his famous work on social psychology, *Human Nature and Conduct* (New York: Henry Holt and Company, 1922).

CHAPTER V

Check Yourself Out

In the first chapter, "When Teachers Talk About Social Studies," we described the plight of Laurie Townsley, a young social studies intern at the mythical Millard Fillmore Junior-Senior High School. Recall Laurie's bewilderment and confusion as each of the social studies staff attempted to help her clarify what social studies "really" ought to be about. By the end of the day, Laurie was totally befuddled, because, first, she could not define the social studies for herself; second, she could not reconcile all the different uses of the "magic" words; and third, she was most uncertain as to her own beliefs. And yet, Laurie sensed that, sooner or later, she would be forced to make a decision--or more accurately, a series of decisions.

Who Wants to be Labeled?

Typically, social studies educators feel just like Laurie--confused as to what is said and what is actually meant. Hardly a sentence is uttered by social studies educators without some reference to the magic words, such as "decision-making," "problems," and "value clarification." Without doubt, educators wish students to think for themselves. Doubtless, no teacher believes that his materials should be "irrelevant." And clearly there is general agreement that students' needs and interests are important, if not paramount. If there is such total agreement as to these magic words, what is the problem?

Throughout this book we have suggested that there are different definitions of social studies and at least three different teaching traditions that seem to flow from these definitions. But, this is not the problem. The problem is that without a common definition or a shared teaching tradition, teachers do become bewildered and confused. Agreeing on the magic words is just not enough, for although the three traditions give some semblance of meaning to these words, there just is not enough direction for teachers who want to know what content to select--what is important, what is irrelevant, how to evaluate results, and how to defend what they do to teachers, administrators, students, and parents.

What we have been saying from the very beginning of this book is that it is important to identify the teaching tradition that seems most compatible to your style. We now anticipate what you would like to say to us: "Why do I have to fall under any of the three traditions? Why do I need to define social studies in the first place? For six decades the field has survived without any overwhelming need to find common understandings. After all, I've got my thing and the other social studies teachers can have theirs. And, anyway, I don't want to be labeled under any of the three traditions. It is barely possible that I can teach quite well without knowing your definition that the 'social studies is the integration of social science and humanities for the purpose of instruction in citizenship education.'" You may even wish to make one more point: "Why not just treat the three traditions like a cafeteria? Lay out the purpose, method, and content of all three and then permit me to select and choose what I want."

If these questions have occured to you, you join hands with many others who have asked identical questions of the authors over the years. We do not intend to duck these questions. In fact, we wish to convince you.

We Would Like to Convince You ...

We would like to convince you that neither Laurie nor you are going to be consistent unless you can recognize social studies as an integration and identify how the three traditions organize and interpret that integration. To be sure, it is possible to approach teaching cafeteria-style, and, in fact, this has been done by teachers for years. But there is a problem. Assume, for a moment, that you buy into the purpose of Reflective Inquiry. Can you also buy into another package that tells you to make certain that students *first* memorize the "right" names, dates, and other pieces of information? And if you say "yes," then there is another question: What will your students say and how will they react when you talk about the need to study problems so that "you can make decisions as a citizen--*but only after you learn the right answers.*" How are you going to select content? Will the content be--as Reflective Inquirers say--those problems which reflect the needs and interests of students? Or will it be that content defined by text or syllabus as essential for students

140

to know? Please don't say both. Finally, how are you going to evaluate? Are you going to use a multiple-choice, short answer test? And if so, how do you defend the position that there really are no very dependable "right" answers out in the real world but you intend to grade on the assumption that there are right answers and the text has them?

One more hypothetical problem: What is going to happen if you find yourself in a school in which the department chairman or dominant teachers are firm believers in social studies taught as social science? You may say to yourself, "Kids need to know how to clarify their values and how to evaluate different positions relative to contemporary problems and issues." But, please be reminded that the heart and soul of the Social Science position emphasizes not *evaluation* but *analysis*. If you announce to your students that they are going to deal with the domain of values, that they are going to express preferences and defend them, what will happen when, in fact, they wind up doing nothing of the sort?

In short, when you stand before your class, utter your first rationale for teaching social studies, ask your first question, make your first test, or give your first grades, you ought to be aware of your own personal set of commitments. If you are not aware of where you stand, you will very probably wind up asking students to do things, to think and to behave in ways that are inconsistent and contradictory. And the first time that your students sense--without being able to articulate elegantly--that you are only mouthing words about "interpreting," "clarifying" or "choosing," they will become cynical, turned-off, resentful, and hostile. And if you think that it is pleasant or even viable to face a classroom of distrustful students who feel that you are being hypocritical, then think again.

Now, after saying all this, would you like to know what social studies tradition you follow? Why not do your students and your colleagues--and your community--a favor and check yourself out? Fill in the following "Social Studies Preference Scale."

If you will take the time to fill out this instrument, we will take the time to try to interpret the results to you.

SOCIAL STUDIES PREFERENCE TABLE

Sample Instructions

The following statements are designed to provide information on how you feel regarding social studies education. You may find yourself agreeing with some statements, disagreeing with others, and being uncertain about still others. Whatever your response, you can be certain that many other people feel the same way that you do.

There are no right or wrong answers to these statements. Rather, your response simply indicates how you feel about each statement. Remember, your response to any statement should indicate how you *usually* feel.

Your response to each statement can range from strongly agree to strongly disagree as follows: 1 = strongly agree (SA); 2 = mostly agree (A); 3 = uncertain (U); 4 = mostly disagree (D); 5 = strongly disagree (SD).

Strongly Agree	Strongly Disagree	
1 2 3 4 5	1.	The principle task of social studies teachers should be to help students assess personal and social value conflicts.
1 2 3 4 5	2.	By internalizing the concepts and methods of the social sciences, students should be able to develop a disciplined mode of analytical thinking.
1 2 3 4 5	3.	Social Science concepts and the scientific method should be used to develop disciplined behavior in the social studies.
1 2 3 4 5	4.	Although our social system is imperfect, students should become citizens who have the moral courage to defend it as the best yet devised by man.
1 2 3 4 5	5.	Students should recognize that teachers and curriculum developers are best qualified to identify the important problems from our social heritage.
1 2 3 4 5	6.	Students can organize their knowledge about social affairs best by using the research procedures and findings of social science authorities.
1 2 3 4 5	7.	Students should develop skills in solving problems which social science scholars have agreed are appropriate for students to pursue.

142

1 2 3 4 5   8. The validity and relevance of content in solving student identified problems can best be judged by the students themselves.

1 2 3 4 5   9. Students who have had the benefit of rigorous in-depth study of problems arising out of the different social science disciplines are more likely to become independent and objective in their analysis of social phenomena.

1 2 3 4 5 10. Although perhaps of limited immediate appeal, students should recognize that knowledge of specifics and values which have stood the test of time will be needed in later life.

1 2 3 4 5 11. The social studies teacher's task is to present the concepts and methodologies of the social science disciplines to students who must then apply these to selected problems.

1 2 3 4 5 12. Teachers should use student ideas to illustrate and reinforce the traditional themes and values which support the best elements of our social heritage.

1 2 3 4 5 13. Sources become authoritative when students and teachers judge them critically in relationship to problems which they sense.

1 2 3 4 5 14. Students should accept the inherent logic of the beliefs, attitudes and values which have molded society.

1 2 3 4 5 15. Students should place their loyalty in the objective and analytical processes of the social sciences rather than the imprecise understandings and feelings of the average person.

1 2 3 4 5 16. Social studies teachers should use student ideas to promote discussions about social issues meaningful to students.

1 2 3 4 5 17. Students should have the moral courage to constantly explore their beliefs, to persevere in their decision, and to alter their decisions based upon reflective judgement.

1 2 3 4 5 18. Students should have the moral courage to defend the methods of social science investigation even when the results obtained run counter to popular opinion.

1 2 3 4 5 19. Social studies teachers should organize their classrooms for the task of acquiring basic information and values.

1 2 3 4 5 20. Social studies teachers should primarily evaluate the ability of students to identify, recall, and recognize basic information and values which are considered essential by society.

143

1 2 3 4 5   21. Students should recognize and accept the principles, generalizations, and values which are essential to the continuance of society.

1 2 3 4 5   22. Social studies teachers should primarily evaluate students on their ability to apply problem solving skills, judge alternative courses of action, and make choices.

1 2 3 4 5   23. Teachers' questions should focus students' attention on recalling important information and values which are essential for becoming a participating adult member of our society.

1 2 3 4 5   23. Students' capacity to become more logical will improve as they sense and identify problems and reflect on the decision-making process inherent in resolving conflicts.

1 2 3 4 5   25. What and how students know arises from investigating problems derived from their own needs and interests.

1 2 3 4 5   26. Students who understand their values and the consequences of their decisions will be better prepared to formulate responsible solutions to personal and social problems.

1 2 3 4 5   27. Legitimate problems can only arise if students sense and perceive conflicts within their own belief and value systems.

1 2 3 4 5   28. Social studies teachers should help students clarify their thinking through reflection about issues which concern them.

1 2 3 4 5   29. Students should become loyal to those ideals from our social heritage which have traditionally offered a large measure of personal freedom and economic opportunity.

1 2 3 4 5   30. The goal of social studies should be to help students recognize and accept the fact that their independence is subject to limitations imposed by their social heritage.

1 2 3 4 5   31. The goal of social studies should be to help students acquire the analytical thinking skills and logic used by social scientists.

1 2 3 4 5   32. The questioning strategies of social studies teachers should be aimed at helping students criticize, test, and evaluate their beliefs about social issues.

1 2 3 4 5   33. To guarantee the continuation of our prized heritage, it is the teacher's task to clarify for students the traditional beliefs upon which our society was founded.

144

1 2 3 4 5   34.   Loyalty should be directed not at a particular set of values or institutions, but to a process which emphasizes reflection upon the students' own needs and interests.

1 2 3 4 5   35.   Constantly refining one's skills in making decisions about personal problems leads to more disciplined behavior.

1 2 3 4 5   36.   Students' understanding of the scientific method can best be developed if they are directly involved in the analysis and interpretation of scientific data.

1 2 3 4 5   37.   Students should learn the basic obligations and responsibilities of good citizenship from their social studies teachers.

1 2 3 4 5   38.   Teachers should use student ideas in formulating and conducting studies similiar to those done by social scientists.

1 2 3 4 5   39.   Students should recognize as sources of authority those text writers and scholars who have selected the most important and enduring values and content for the social studies.

1 2 3 4 5   40.   Students should discipline their behavior to conform with certain basic information and values.

1 2 3 4 5   41.   Student progress can best be assessed by how well they apply social science concepts and methodology to problems novel to them.

1 2 3 4 5   42.   Students who regularly engage in reflection on problems of their own choosing should become more independent in their thinking and actions.

1 2 3 4 5   43.   Clarifying relationships of social science concepts should be the focus of questioning strategies employed by social studies teachers.

1 2 3 4 5   44.   Students who use social science concepts and the social science method will probably formulate and propose responsible decisions.

1 2 3 4 5   45.   Teachers should clarify both the generalizations and processes of the social sciences for students who will perceive their importance in the future.

The Matrix

Instructions:

Each of the statements you have marked has a corresponding number in the matrix below. Place the rating number you have circled next to the statement number in the matrix. For example: if on statement number 1 you strongly disagreed (circled 5), place 5 next to number 1 in the place provided in the matrix. Finish filling in your ratings in the matrix until all 45 items are completed. When you have done this, see further instructions below.

	Social Studies as Citizenship Transmission	Social Studies as Social Science	Social Studies as Reflective Inquiry
Purpose	4.......... 14.......... 29.......... 30.......... 37.......... cell total_____	9.......... 15.......... 18.......... 31.......... 44.......... cell total_____	17.......... 24.......... 26.......... 34.......... 42.......... cell total_____
Method	12.......... 19.......... 20.......... 23.......... 33.......... cell total_____	11.......... 38.......... 41.......... 43.......... 45.......... cell total_____	1.......... 16.......... 22.......... 28.......... 32.......... cell total_____
Content	5.......... 10.......... 21.......... 39.......... 40.......... cell total_____	2.......... 3.......... 6.......... 7.......... 36.......... cell total_____	8.......... 13.......... 25.......... 27.......... 35.......... cell total_____
	pattern total _____	pattern total _____	pattern total _____

Further instructions:

Total your ratings in each cell at the place marked "cell total." When you have each of the cell totals, add together the three cell totals in each column for the "pattern total." Add the purpose, method, and content cell totals under the column marked Social Studies as Citizenship Transmission and then under the remaining two columns.

Interpreting Your Matrix

Work on interpreting each cell total first. The general rule is that the lower your total score, the more strongly you agree with the statements in the cell and, conversely, the higher the number, the more strongly you disagree with the statement, For example, the strongest *total agree* in any cell would be 5, the strongest *total disagree* would be 25. To interpret the strength of agreement in any of the cells, compare your score with the following:

a). 5 to 9   strongly agree
b). 10 to 15   slightly agree
c). 16 to 20   slightly disagree
d). 21 to 25   strongly disagee

To interpret your pattern totals, compare your pattern totals with the following:

a). 15 to 30   strongly agree
b). 31 to 45   slightly agree
c). 46 to 60   slightly disagree
d). 51 to 75   strongly disagree

By now you have interpreted your own scores in each of the cells and in each of the patterns. Your scores may suggest that you clearly favor one position over another. But if your scores are similar to those of the majority of elementary and secondary teachers and graduate students who have used this preference scale, then your scores suggest that you are not consistent. For example, you might find that you strongly agree with one position and yet also strongly agree with the other two. Some have marked strong agreement with purpose and method but disagreement with content in a particular position. The fact is that almost no two patterns are exactly alike. However, having tested this preference scale on both students and teachers from selected universities, and elementary and secondary teachers, six patterns of response have emerged. Would you like to compare your response with those of the six general patterns that most often appear? If so, then examine the following patterns to find the one that most closely resembles your own tradition. To the right of each "typical" pattern we have provided you with a brief explanation, noting some of the possible implications.

1. *Reflective Inquiry Pattern:*
Of every 100 who marked the scale, around 20 show patterns consistent with this illustration. Notice that the cell totals under CT and SS suggest strong disagreement where those under RI show strong agreement. If your responses are similar to this matrix, this suggests that you see clear differences in the various social studies tradtions and maintain a very consistent Reflective Inquiry position. This pattern suggests that the purpose of citizenship is rational decision-making and that the proper method to arrive at decision-making is the Reflective Inquiry process, and that you believe that the content for your course should arise with the needs and interests identified by students.

	Citizenship Transmission CT	Social Science SS	Reflective Inquiry RI
purpose	slightly disagree	strongly disagree	strongly agree
method	strongly disagree	slightly disagree	strongly agree
content	strongly disagree	strongly disagree	strongly agree
pattern totals	strongly disagree	strongly disagree	strongly agree

2. *Reflective Inquiry and Social Science Pattern:*

Of those who marked the check-out, approximately 20% chose to follow this pattern. This pattern suggests that citizenship transmission is not acceptable but that you are not distinguishing between SS and RI. This pattern shows that you beieve the purpose of citizenship education is decision-making. But your choice of method suggests that you would approve problem-solving, though you're not sure whether it should be Reflective Inquiry or discovery, etc. Your're not settled on where content should be identified. You believe content should meet the needs and interests of students but you're not sure where content should come from.

	Citizenship Transmission CT	Social Science SS	Reflective Inquiry RI
purpose	slightly disagree	slightly agree	slightly agree
method	slightly agree	slightly agree	slightly agree
content	slightly agree	slightly agree	slightly agree
pattern totals	slightly disagree	slightly agree	slightly agree

3. *Citizenship Transmission and Reflective Inquiry Pattern:*

Somewhat fewer than 10% of those who used this scale chose this pattern. This pattern seems to show a rejection of SS but acceptance of CT and RI. To agree with both traditions demonstrates conflicting beliefs. The two traditions are contradictory. RI calls for a decision-making process based upon student needs and interests; CT is based upon authoritarian interpretations transmited as essential values. If you follow this pattern, you might well experience difficulties in making decisions on purpose, method, and content.

	Citizenship Transmission CT	Social Science SS	Reflective Inquiry RI
purpose	slightly agree	slightly agree	slightly agree
method	slightly agree	slightly disagree	slightly agree
content	strongly agree	slightly disagree	slightly disagree
pattern totals	slightly agree	slightly disagree	slightly agree

4. *Citizenship Transmission and Social Science and Reflective Inquiry Pattern:*

Approximately 30% marking the scale followed this pattern. It is interesting to note that no students actually disagreed with the RI position. Part of the explanation for this is "word magic." Inquiry, decision-making, and needs and interests are undefined; thus they can be agreed to by anyone. This pattern suggests general acceptance of all the different points of view at once. Everything sounds good even though the "goods" are inconsistent. As is true in the above pattern, you might experience a great deal of indecision about your purpose, method, and content.

	Citizenship Transmission CT	Social Science SS	Reflective Inquiry RI
purpose	slightly agree	slightly agree	strongly agree
method	slightly disagree	slightly agree	slightly agree
content	slightly agree	slightly agree	slightly agree
pattern totals	slightly agree	slightly agree	slightly agree

5. *Citizenship Transmission Pattern:*

A very small percentage, probably less than 10%, select this pattern. You should note that this is unusual because as we have said previously, CT is by far the tradition most frequently practiced. If you followed this pattern, you probably believe in a citizenship that calls for the inculcation of basic values. Most likely, your method will be that of transmitting content with textbook, recitation, lecture, question and answer, and a commitment to ground-covering. Finally, this pattern suggests that you will depend heavily upon your interpretation of selected events which students will be expected to note.

If you have selected this pattern, you should have litle difficulty in making logical decisions for you have chosen a consistent pattern.

	Citizenship Transmission CT	Social Science SS	Reflective Inquiry RI
purpose	strongly agree	slightly disagree	slightly disagree
method	strongly agree	slightly disagree	strongly disagree
content	strongly agree	slightly disagree	strongly disagree
pattern totals	strongly agree	slightly disagree	strongly disagree

6. *Social Science Pattern:*

This pattern, which favors teaching social studies as social science, is selected by approximately 10% of all those marking the preference scale. As we have said previously, many social studies educators do not clearly discriminate between the SS and RI traditions. Therefore, there is a substantial group of students who draw from both traditions. However, if you follow this pattern, you probably believe that social studies means a liberal arts interpretation of citizenship; that is, there is general knowledge that informed men should have. In this case, the general knowledge should be the structure of social science disciplines with emphasis upon discovery learning. It follows that you believe that the problems to be studied are those identified by professional social scientists. If you have selected this pattern, you should have little difficulty in making logical decisions for you have chosen a consistent pattern.

	Citizenship Transmission CT	Social Science SS	Reflective Inquiry RI
purpose	strongly disagree	strongly agree	slightly disagree
method	strongly disagree	strongly agree	strongly agree
content	slightly disagree	strongly agree	slightly disagree
pattern totals	strongly disagree	strongly agree	slightly disagree

What is your position? Does it matter?

What position you own is between you and your conscience. Any of the three traditions is defensible, rational, and culturally acceptable--at least in some sense. If you hold with one of the traditions and generally hold it consistently and act consistently in terms of that tradition, then you have a basis upon which to make meaningful, consistent classroom decisions about purpose, method, and content. In other words, you have a set of standards by which to guide your teaching decisions.

151

Now, what if you are one of the 30-40% who hold mixed positions, that is, what if you seem to be buying all the positions at once? We believe that you are opening yourself up to some of the problems we have described--your students will not know what to expect. You will talk one way, make another kind of assignment, and evaluate students on yet a third basis. However, there is nothing that says that you are fated to be inconsistent and your teaching confused. You can avoid confusion in your thinking and inconsistancy in your practice by becoming aware of the relationship between your beliefs about teaching and the practices that flow from them.

We argue that if you "know where you are coming from," that is, if you can identify both your goals and the means by which you reach goals, you will be more likely to plan, select content, arrange strategies, and evaluate with a greater likelihood of success. Your students will soon learn what to expect from you. You will avoid the charge of hypocrisy and inconsistency. And you will probably gain a deeper sense of satisfaction from teaching.

In the end it is not a question of whether you wish to be labeled or whether or not you will be required to make decisions. As a teacher you will make decisions. Making independent and autonomous decisions in the face of novel circumstances happens to be the definition of a profession. Further, whether you believe it or not, you do in fact have the freedom to make many decisions. That is what the term "academic freedom" means.

If choice is inevitable, then just what is the issue? The issue revolves around the kind of teacher you eventually wish to be, what you really want to accomplish, what you stand for, and what type of professional you wish to grow into. If you can identify what choices you face, if you know the consequences of choice, you can become pretty much what you want to become. That is the point of this book. That is the point of teaching.